I0087201

THE WAY OF THE RIVER

THE WAY OF THE RIVER

My Journey of Fishing, Forgiveness and Spiritual Recovery

Randy Kadish

Saw Mill River Press

The Way of the River:
My Journey of Fishing, Forgiveness and Spiritual Recovery
Copyright © 2012 by Randy Kadish

Saw Mill River Press
Ansonia Station
P.O. Box 230675
New York, NY 10023

All rights reserved. No part of this book may be used or reproduced in any manner whatsoever including Internet usage, without written permission of the author.

ISBN-13: 978-0615706795
ISBN-10: 0615706797

Book design by Maureen Cutajar
www.gopublished.com

For all those who have been too numb to cry.

In loving memory of my loving grandmother,
Ada Panken, and my aunt, Anna Baer.

CONTENTS

INTRODUCTION

I never set out to write a book about my journey of fishing and of spiritual and emotional recovery. In fact, I never set out to write any of what follows. As ideas came to me—I didn't look for any of them—I wrote, one memoir, one autobiographical story at a time. It was only after I unexpectedly went through a life-changing crisis that I came to see that my memoirs and stories told much of my often difficult, often gratifying journey and were meant to go together. They do not, however, tell a seamless story. Instead, they tell a story with some holes, as well as meanderings and changes of directions. Perhaps that's how it should be. After all, that is the way of rivers and of recovery.

PROLOGUE

My sister's boyfriend, Paul, called and told me my sister had fainted in her doctor's office and had been rushed, in an ambulance, to a hospital in South Florida.

"She may have a bad case of pneumonia," Paul said. "She was having trouble breathing."

"Can I call her?"

"She's in the ICU. They don't have phones in there."

"It must be serious. Can I call her doctor?"

"Yes, here's his phone number."

I called and left a message. About a half hour later he called back and confirmed my sister's condition was serious.

"She waited too long to see me," he said. "I'll keep you updated on her condition."

I wanted to fly down and visit her. I thought of my financial hole, but told myself I'd take off from work and charge the airline tickets to my credit card. "I can get down there tomorrow."

"It's probably best you don't come right now. She needs rest. She's heavily sedated because of the tube we put down her throat. I'll tell her you called."

I thanked the doctor and then thought, *Please, Sharon, don't die. Please. If our mother and father were alive they too would want you to live.* I closed my eyes and remembered that for so long I didn't care whether my sister, a drug addict, lived or died, and how for so long all I saw in her were lies and selfishness. *Today I see her so differently. Today I see her as someone who, like me, was often beaten and yelled at and never listened to. But unlike me, the first male in my family who lived, she was not the favorite of the family. No wonder she felt jealous and resentful of me, and suffered from severe depression. If only I had known sooner what depression really is. Now, partly because of my unexpected crisis, I finally know why my sister and others turn to drugs and alcohol.*

Two very long—for me—days later my sister's doctor called and told me she was out of danger. Grateful, very grateful, I thought back to when we were children and tried to make jelly apples by spreading jam on them and then putting them into the freezer. It didn't work, and instead fueled another one of my mother's violent rages. *How different life for me and Sharon would have been if not for all those rages. But then would I have ever been forced to take my journey that restored my sanity?* I thought about how my journey was emotional and spiritual—an uphill, winding journey that began by accident when I finally admitted I couldn't communicate and had to ask for help, a journey that probably saved my life, and that I therefore often wrote about, hoping to give back something positive to the universe, something to help ease the suffering of people in pain.

I went to my desk, opened a drawer and took out the stack of my memoirs and autobiographical stories. I thought of the Grateful Dead lyrics, "What a long strange journey it's been."

Could it be my difficult childhood and my endless disappointments were meant to be and happened for a reason? It doesn't seem possible.

But maybe, just maybe, it is.

I took out a red pen and started editing and rewriting.

DIFFERENT LEVELS OF FISHING AND...

For the first time in three years I dialed her number. My mother answered the phone. I tried to speak, but my words, like a snagged fly, got stuck inside me.

"Hello," my mother repeated.

I freed my words. "It's, it's me."

"Randy! It's so good to—My mother cried. Her tears swelled my guilt and drowned my voice. A long silence. My mother asked if I still drove a limousine. I remembered how she'd always yearned for me to become a doctor. Knowing my answer would pain her, I admitted I still drove.

Another silence. I hoped she would ask if I still wrote. She didn't. So I told her I had published several fishing articles.

"Fishing? I didn't know you were that into it."

"During the last few years I've been."

"I'm glad you found something you like," she said sincerely, so sincerely I again hoped that she would apologize, finally.

She didn't. She asked to meet, but didn't offer the apology I wanted to hear. I told her I wasn't ready to, but promised to call again.

"I've—I've missed you so," she said. I hung up, wondering if something was wrong with me because I couldn't forgive her. Like an opened dam, my questions let loose a rushing river of guilt inside me. Again, I tried to understand the violence of my childhood, and then the violence of war. No answers came, not once during the long, cold winter and the early spring.

I packed for my fishing trip to the Beaverkill. Eleanor, who worked for my mother's employment agency, called. Her words iced all my feelings. I hung up, called the owner of the Roscoe Motel, apologized, and said I had to cancel my reservation. He said he understood and would refund my deposit.

An hour later, feeling I was in a trance, I walked down a white hospital hallway. At first the long hallway reminded me of a straight, narrow stream, but suddenly the hallway seemed like the opposite of a stream. It was colorless and lifeless, and made me feel boxed in. I looked straight ahead. Instead of seeing a beautiful, gurgling run or a long, slow pool, I saw an open doorway. On the other side, my mother sat on a bed. She wore a floppy beach hat. I walked into her room. She looked at me and smiled. "Do you like my hat?" she asked. "It's not exactly Saks Fifth Avenue."

"Yes, I like it." I thought even without hair, she was still beautiful.

"Now I know why some men wear even bad toupees." My mother laughed, momentarily. "I never thought I could get cancer, me, a woman who built her own business from the ground up. Are you sure you don't want the business?"

I thought of saying yes and making her happy, but then thought, *It's taken me so long to get published. Do I really want to give up writing?* I said, "I'm sorry, but your business is not for me."

The doctor walked in. He was tall, probably in his late fifties. He wore a dark pinstripe suit and looked more like a banker than a doctor. He motioned me to follow him out of the room. I did. He told me cancer was unpredictable, but in his opinion, my mother had about three months to live.

Not believing him, I asked, "How could this be happening?"

"I wish I had an answer. Your mother is very proud of you. I once wished I had the courage to become a writer."

I thought it was ironic that my mother was always impressed by doctors, and now her doctor was impressed by writers.

"What do you write about?" he asked.

"Fishing."

I expected him to laugh. He didn't.

"When I was a boy," he said, "I loved fishing with my father. But when I got older I resented that fishing seemed more important to him than I did, so I turned my back on fishing, until he got cancer. We fished together several times before he died. I'm so grateful we did."

"I wish I could fish with my mother, but she was never the outdoor type."

"Neither am I, but lately I've been thinking of getting into fly fishing and spending more time with myself. Fly fishing looks so beautiful and peaceful."

Suddenly, he looked like a fly fisher, but to me so did almost everyone. I said, "In the beginning fly fishing can be very frustrating, like golf."

"I've heard fly fishing is a real art."

"Well, then I guess I paint by numbers. In my opinion, the beauty of fly fishing is that you can do it at different levels. Some anglers always try to match the hatch and are always changing flies and leaders, but a few anglers, well they're less scientific. They fish to experience the beauty of nature. I remember meeting this old guy on the Beaverkill who fished only what we call an attractor fly, an Adams. He said that if he caught a few less fish than more so-called scientific anglers did, would it really matter when all was said and done?"

"What kind of fly fisher are you?"

I thought a moment. "I'm relatively new to fly fishing, so I'm still not really sure. I guess right now I'm a little of everything."

He smiled. "I like what you said about fishing on different levels. Sometimes I wish I could be a doctor on different levels, but if I did, well, it wouldn't be fair to my patients. How much would I have to spend for a good fly rod?"

"The technology has advanced so much that you can get something good for around three hundred dollars, maybe even less."

We shook hands. I walked back into the room.

"What did the doctor say?" my mother asked.

Not wanting to tell her the whole truth, I walked to the window and told her we talked about fishing.

"Fishing, that's all?"

"Yes, he's interested in getting back into it." Outside the setting sun colored the East River orange and the sky pink. The orange reminded me of blood, the pink of flesh, and in my mind, the river became a big vein. I looked downstream, saw a fishing boat and realized that big, straight rivers could be as beautiful as winding trout streams. Suddenly, smoke streamed out of the huge chimneys of the Con Edison plant and dirtied the sky. Still I said, "What a view you have."

"It's not so great," my mother disagreed.

Not arguing back, I stared at the river and wondered if, in the fall, I should buy a saltwater fly rod and fish the river for stripers. After all, I didn't live so far away. Besides, big rivers were a lot closer in shape and beauty to trout streams than to hospital hallways. *With my mother so sick, is this the time to think about fishing or to reflect on rivers? Am I a bad son after all?*

I walked to my mother. For the first time since I was fourteen I touched her. She grabbed my hand.

I fought back tears and said, "I'm so, so sorry for not calling you for so long. Maybe if I had you wouldn't be here."

"No one knows why people get cancer. I want you to promise me that you won't blame yourself."

"I wish I could."

"You have so much of your life ahead of you. Besides, being sick is worth having you in my life again."

I lied and said, "You're going to be all right."

"We'll see. Your sister would love to hear from you."

I thought of how my sister often stole and lied about her drug use, and of how my family always rewarded her by giving her money, money she spent on drugs. I thought of how my family often told me that my sister was wonderful, and that I should be a better brother to her. I said, "I'm just not ready to call her."

"Well maybe soon. In the meantime, I want to read your articles."

"I don't think you'll like them. Most are about casting fishing rods. One is about fly fishing the Bronx and Saw Mill Rivers."

"I still want to see you what you wrote," she insisted.

The next day I showed her two of my articles. She looked at one of the photos. "Is that you?" she asked.

"Yes. I'm fishing a pool in the Saw Mill River."

"What a beautiful picture."

"I used a tripod and took it myself."

"I love your fly fishing hat. Can you get me one?"

"Sure." I left the hospital, went to Orvis and bought my mother a hat. The next day when she tried it on I held up a mirror. She looked at her reflection and smiled.

"I love it," she said. "Too bad we can't fish together."

"Maybe soon we can."

"I'm a klutz. Besides, don't wait for me. If the weather's nice I want you to take a break from visiting and go fishing."

The next day was beautiful, but I didn't feel like fishing, until I became desperate to get my mind off my mother's illness and off the thought that I had probably caused it by detaching from her with an ax. I rode the train up to Westchester, climbed down a steep bank, and waded into the Saw Mill River, a stream I had described in an article as having pools as varied and as beautiful as any pools in Montana or Idaho. I tied on a streamer and fished it straight downstream, toward the big, fallen tree. In spite of what I had written, I didn't see the Saw Mill's beauty. I didn't see, for example, its high, mosaic-like roof meshed together with long branches and sun-brightened leaves. Instead, I saw only my mother lying in a hospital bed. Why? Was it because years before when I was a desperate-to-be-published writer I had unintentionally exaggerated the stream's beauty to make my article more marketable? Or was it because a part of me, a big part, no longer felt I deserved to see beauty and to feel close to it? Abruptly, I waded out of the stream, climbed up the steep bank, and walked to the train station.

A week or so later, I accidentally saw a medical ad for a new cancer treatment. Two weeks later my mother underwent a new kind of surgery: radiosurgery. Her tumors shrank. My lies about her getting better became the truth. Grateful, I often visited my mother and held her hand—my way of apologizing—and I became what she had always wanted me to become: a loving son. I couldn't, however, bring myself to call my sister, especially after I ran into her in the hospital and saw she was stoned again.

A year later tumors erupted in my mother's brain. Day after day I held her hand and told her a new truth: "I love you, and I'm grateful for all the good things you tried to do for me, grateful you're my mother."

She squeezed my hand. I squeezed back.

My mother grew thinner and soon turned into a flesh-covered skeleton. But she never blamed me for her cancer. One day she said, "You should write a book."

"I've already tried, many times, but no one wanted them."

"You can't let the past write the future."

Surprised at my mother's insightful comment, I said, "So you don't mind me trying to become a real writer?"

"As long as it's what you want."

"Well for now I'm happy writing fishing articles and getting published."

"I want you to be happy. Can I ask you something?"

"Yes."

"After I'm gone can you promise me you'll call your sister once a week?"

"You're not dying."

"We all are. Will you promise?"

"Yes, I promise."

My mother smiled and squeezed my hand.

A week later she died. I expected to fall into a quicksand of grief, but the strange thing was I didn't. I wondered why. Perhaps her illness had given me a lot of time to come to terms with life and her passing, but then I wondered if I was just too terrified to face an ugly truth: My detachment was the cause of my mother's death.

So I was looking for an escape. I found it by writing a story about an innocent angler who grows up fly fishing and cherishing the beauty of the Beaverkill River. World War Two erupts like a cancer, and the angler feels he wants to fight evil. He enlists. After the war he returns as a different person.

I put the story away, but during the next few months it grew in my mind and turned into a novel, mostly about the angler's father, Ian, a man who can't make peace with the world, and who retreats into fishing and into teaching literature. Afraid of conflict, he wonders if he's a coward. Eventually, so does his son, Everett. Ashamed of his father, Everett enlists. Angry and afraid of losing Everett, Ian blames himself and a senseless, war-filled world. Years later, after experiencing more tragedy, Ian learns to accept a world he can't understand, and to see beauty in nature and in man's great discoveries, such as new medical technology.

I finished a first draft of the book. Proud, feeling like I was doing what my mother wanted, I decided to reward myself by taking a short trip to the Beaverkill.

The next day I drove to my favorite pool: Barnhart's. I looked upstream at the fast, riffled mouth. I looked downstream at the slow, smooth tail. In the pool I saw a reflection of my mother: a once-raging woman who, because of cancer, finally calmed in the tail years of her life. Suddenly I was grateful that rivers couldn't get tumors and wither and die, grateful that, thanks to nature's way, rivers, like history, were stronger than men and women. *Is it the strength, the eternity of this river that is now bringing me back to fishing? Am I hoping to borrow, in some way, strength from the river?*

I walked along the bank toward the pool's tail. I thought of how the pool played a small but important part in my book. I wondered if rivers, like actors, could really play parts other than the ones nature assigned them. Wading into the river, I thought of how beautiful Barnhart's looked in spite of the highway on top of its high bank, and of how the river's other pools—Ferdon's, Covered Bridge, Junction—were probably equally beautiful. I thought of how the Westchester streams I fished were, in their way, as beautiful as the Beaverkill.

But if rivers can be beautiful on very different levels, does it mean that rivers that aren't so beautiful don't have as much of a reason to exist?

No, I answered.

I didn't see a hatch. I opened one of my fly boxes and stared at about thirty different nymphs. Suddenly I remembered what I had told my mother's doctor about how fishing can be done on different levels. I opened another fly box, picked out an Adams and tied it on. I pulled line off my reel and cast to the far bank. My line and fly splashed simultaneously on the water. Though my cast was less than perfect, I thought I could still get a good drift. I mended, watched my Adams float downstream and wondered if boys and men could be sons and brothers on different levels, and, no matter what level they chose, be equally okay. Something, maybe my mother's recent passing, told me no.

My line bowed downstream. It was too late to mend. I retrieved line and again cast, this time slightly downstream.

The front of my unrolling line landed on the water. My Adams turned over and gently floated down.

Again I watched my Adams. *Yes, I have made mistakes that I wish I could erase or fix like a bad cast; but at least I was with my mother all through her long illness. At least, I have come to see that she, like the hero of my novel, did the best she could, and so did I. And thankfully, I have also come to see that apologizing is like fishing. We can choose to do it on different levels?*

AFTERMATH

I kept the promise I made to my mother and called my sister once a week. Making the calls wasn't easy. Several times my sister slurred her words, so I assumed she was high. Something, however, told me not to ask if she was. Besides her being high, what pained me was her never listening to me. For example, one day, I told her I had changed jobs and was worried because I wouldn't have health insurance for three months.

"Medicaid is making me pay more for my drugs," my sister said. "My anti-depressants are costing me ten dollars more a month."

I felt like saying, "What are you complaining about? You almost never worked a day in your life, and most of your medical bills are paid."

Is it any wonder I always tried to end my conversations with her as quickly as possible. I believed I didn't owe my sister anything. I wanted to detach from her—again with an ax, but because of the promise I had made to my mother, I didn't.

One day at work I happened to mention to someone how painful talking to my sister was. My coworker suggested that I try going to a Twelve Step meeting, where I would get advice on how to stop my sister from using drugs.

A few days later I went to my first meeting. Feeling very nervous, I walked into a big room filled with about forty people. Hanging in the front of the room was a chart of the Twelve Steps. I read them. The first thing about the Steps I didn't like was the idea of believing in God. If there were a God, I couldn't understand why He had abandoned me in a violent, dysfunctional home, and why He had abandoned mankind to a succession of bloody wars.

The second thing about the Steps I didn't like was the idea of me making amends. After all, it was my sister, not me, who used drugs, who lied and stole. She had caused me so much pain; why should I make amends to her? I hadn't harmed her. She had harmed me. The Steps just didn't make sense.

I thought, *I'm probably in the wrong place.*

I took a seat anyway, and listened as person after person spoke about staying in the moment, keeping the focus on themselves, not regretting the past, etc. No one, however, said anything about how to stop someone from drinking or drugging.

Abruptly I left the meeting, expecting someone to follow me out and try to persuade me to return. No one did. I was sure I would never go back.

For two months I didn't.

Then grief hit me like a punch. The pain was as physical as much as it was emotional. It seemed to cut through me like a big dull blade. For the first time in my life I suffered from headaches.

I assumed the grief would run its course and soon retreat, but instead it dug in, pushing deeper and deeper into me, then spreading through me like some sort of heavy liquid. At times I felt I couldn't move, especially in the morning when I woke up. Again and again I had to remind myself that I had to get out of bed and go to work, and that I was better off being with people than with myself.

Desperate for help, I finally called my old therapist, Matt, and started seeing him once a week. Often I told him I felt responsible for my mother's death, and was furious at myself for not forgiving my mother before she got cancer. Day after day I wished I could wade downstream in the years of my life and rewrite my past. Matt tried to help me come to terms with my guilt, and reminded me that my mother had been a violent, difficult person who never apologized or listened to me. According to him, therefore, I shouldn't blame myself.

"Loving, functional parents also get cancer," Matt said.

The weekly therapy sessions didn't end my pain, but they kept me afloat, so to speak, but just barely. Besides feeling guilty, I felt terribly lonely, especially on Saturday nights. During my mother's long illness many of my old friends—some of them alcoholics—had stopped calling me. (I had assumed they didn't want to hear about terminal cancer.) Desperate to break out of my isolation, I reluctantly went back to the Twelve Step meeting. Always I sat in the back of the room. Never did I raise my hand and speak. I just didn't feel as if I belonged, even though I kind of liked being with people whose childhoods had been as traumatic as mine.

Then one evening an African-American woman told the story of how she had always reacted to and lashed out at her alcoholic family until finally, after years of recovery, she learned to stop reacting and to start living her own life.

Her words set something off inside me. Her story, I knew, was also my story. Though I still didn't want to believe in God or to make amends, I bought a copy of the meeting list and started going to three or four meetings a week.

Though a God didn't grant me serenity, my grief slowly eased.

It was spring. I thought of fishing, but still weighed down by grief, I didn't have the energy to fish. Then one day I couldn't bear being alone in my apartment. I grabbed my fly-fishing gear, walked to the old broken-down pier off West 55th Street and fished. Right from the start I felt comforted by nature, so I returned to the pier twice a week or so, and soon I got the idea of making an amends to my mother by writing a memoir about my fishing from the pier and coming to terms with her passing, but something, maybe my fear of reliving my guilt kept me from writing.

The cold winds of early winter came and ended my trips to the pier. I was scared that, without the serenity I had found there,

I'd again feel the dull cutting blade of grief.

The winds became colder and stronger. I sat in a car waiting for my clients. Seemingly out of nowhere, the first line of a memoir about my coming to terms with my mother's death popped into my mind. I took out the small notebook I always carried in my briefcase, and wrote down the line—then a second line, and a third. Suddenly, the words flowed like a fast stream. I couldn't stop them. In about an hour I finished a draft. During the next month I often revised it. Finally, I submitted it to three or four magazines. They rejected it. Discouraged, I submitted it to The FlyFisher, a magazine with a small circulation but with a long, prestigious past. A few days later the editor, Dick Wentz, called me and offered me seventy-five dollars for the memoir. Of course I accepted, not knowing then that it would be the first of many memoirs and autobiographical stories I would write.

A REASON TO FISH

The city workers never stopped me from going onto the old, broken-down pier, though one had said, "There aren't many fish here since we dredged last year."

I often sought comfort in those words. They told me not to blame myself for catching only one striped bass after so many months of trying.

So with few expectations, I again walked towards the end of the seagull-inhabited pier on an autumn day. One by one the beautiful birds spread their long, gray wings and soared away. I was sorry I had frightened them from their home.

I continued on.

On the New Jersey side of the wide, fast-moving river the fluttering American flag told me the wind blew from the north, but not strongly. Because strong winds were the only thing I didn't like about fishing, I was thankful, and wondered if I should go with a floating or sinking line.

I checked the sky. The cloud cover was breaking up. I chose a sinking line, knowing it probably wouldn't matter. I set up my nine-weight rod, looked through my fly box and wondered, *What should I try? A Clouser? A Deceiver?*

I tied on a White Deceiver. On the other end of the pier sea-gulls gracefully glided down and landed. Glad they had returned, I thought, *If only I could get my fly to land as gently.* I cast up river, about 70 feet. *Not bad.* Trying to mimic an injured bait fish, I stripped erratically—slowly, then quickly, and pausing every four or five seconds.

Suddenly, as if a light switch had been turned on, the sun

broke through a small opening in the clouds and illuminated the gold and raspberry-red leaves of some of the New Jersey trees. *Yes, autumn is always the prettiest time to fish. But soon those trees will look like eerie, mushroom-shaped spider webs. Soon it will be winter and too cold to fish. So why on this mild day am I the only one here? Is it because, unlike most anglers, I'm not so obsessed with catching fish? If so, is there something wrong with me? Am I less of an angler?*

A small motor boat approached. A middle-aged couple was aboard. They held hands, reminding me that I hadn't held a woman's hand since I had learned my mother had brain cancer.

I waved to the couple. They smiled and waved back.

"Any luck?" the man yelled out.

I shook my head no and remembered that I never felt alone on the pier.

I again cast. The front of my fly line formed a tight loop and cut through the breeze. Eighty feet away my Deceiver turned over perfectly and landed softly on the water. I was proud. *Yes, maybe basking in the satisfaction of making a good cast is what brought me to the pier. But is there something more?*

I lowered my rod, pulled all the slack out of my line, and tried to repeat my beautiful cast. My back cast loop was tight. When it almost unrolled I slowly began my forward cast. *Perfect.* I accelerated into my power snap. I hauled, but too late and not fast enough. My forward cast loop was wide. The breeze knocked it down. My fly barely turned over. The front of my line landed in a small pile. Disappointed, I quickly retrieved line until it was straight. Again I erratically retrieved. *Maybe bad casts really aren't so bad. Maybe a fish will still strike. Besides, my next cast will be better, I hope. Yes, to make better: how good it always feels, and how easy to do when fishing. If only fixing my executive search business had been so easy, but by the time I realized that the market had changed it was too late. And by the time Mother realized that her cough might be a sign of something really serious it was also too late. By then even the latest medical breakthroughs couldn't stop the cancer from eating away at her, from leaving her a living, breathing skeleton, and leaving me feeling helpless and furious at a God who seemed brutal and cruel. Why did he cause so much pain? So much suffering!?*

I looked up at the dirty-grey, cloud-covered sky and again tried to answer the questions. I couldn't, the same way I couldn't back then when, after my mother's passing, each moment became a link on a chain gang of grief. I couldn't find the energy to fish. Soon my apartment seemed like a dungeon. Then the walls became a vise and started closing in. Afraid I was losing my mind, I knew I had to escape. I wondered, *but to where?* A voice told me to take my fly rod and reel. I didn't want to listen, at first, but then I took my fly rod out of its case. It seemed to shine like gold. I held the rod handle. The cork felt like silk. It comforted me. I went to my closet, put on my fly-fishing vest, and looked in the mirror. *Yes, I was once an angler. Yes, once I loved being in the outdoors, especially in a gurgling river or a gently crashing surf.*

I took my fly fishing rod and reel, trudged to the old pier, and again I became an angler. Surprisingly, my grief numbed, or maybe even lifted. The next day I again went to the pier; and before long fishing was all I really cared about.

Finally, slowly, my other interests—football, music, history—returned, but none rivaled fishing on the pier, even if I had on the wrong fly.

I looked down from the sky, toward the murky water, and wondered if I should change flies. Soon I decided that, in the scheme of things—with nature's vast beauty embracing me, soothing me in a way that my mother never did—the question of what fly I should have on seemed terribly small. *I'll stay with the White Deceiver. Just remember that, just before my back cast unrolls, I should shoot line and break my wrist and drift my fly rod down.*

I cast. My forward loop tightened and streaked like an arrow. My fly turned over and landed about 90 feet away. I smiled. Above the middle of the river a flock of seagulls circled. Their sharp chirps somehow sounded amplified by the peaceful vision of the orange sun, setting but still beaming down onto the gently flowing river and shattering into hundreds of bobbing and reflecting diamonds.

The seagulls didn't dive. Bait fish probably weren't around, so neither were the striped bass.

I wasn't discouraged. So for the next half hour, as the sky ripened, like fruit, into dark pink, I cast and retrieved again and again, afraid only that the sun would soon sink behind the far bank and roll up the long, flickering path that seemed to end at my pier.

Slow down. Don't worry about the sun going down. It will be here tomorrow, and so will I. And don't worry about winter. Before long it will retreat and the bare trees will again bloom with life, and then maybe the stripers will return to the pier, but if they don't, will it really matter?

No, because out here nothing is broken, except fixable casts.

CITY ANGLER

I am a city angler.

I was born in a city, and grew up and live in a city. I fish in a city or in rivers that are near train stations; so when I walk down the street or ride the subways, carrying fly-fishing gear, wearing an official fly-fishing vest, and also galoshes over my felt-soled wading boots, people stare and probably wonder: Is he an alien?

No, I'm not, I know.

I'm just someone on his way to Grand Central Station, where I'll buy a train ticket and a slice of Junior's cheesecake, and ride the rails up to Croton Falls and fish the Croton River.

The branches of the river flow into a big pool about a hundred yards behind the small village. The pool reminds me of the famous Junction Pool on the Beaverkill River, but the Croton Falls pool is not famous; and neither am I, though I once wanted to be.

I stepped off the train. Because the Croton River is fly-fishing paradise for many, no one in the town stared at me. I was sort of invisible. Thankful, I wondered, *Where should I fish? The big pool? The shallow, rocky riffles of the East Branch? The long, long, slow pool of the lower West Branch? What about the classic dry-fly water of the upper West Branch?*

The entire West Branch, I knew, was popular with the anglers who formed what I called The Croton Falls Fishing Club.

But I was from the city and not a member.

I put on my waders, set up my seven-foot, four-weight rod and thought, *It's a weekday. The upper stretch of the river shouldn't be too crowded. Besides, I can walk on the path alongside the river, and easily find open water. And if the stretch is crowded, well, aren't I a little lonely?*

I crossed the footbridge, then Route 100. I turned left on Butlerville Road. Only three cars were parked near the bridge over Garcia Pool. Most of the river, I knew, would be mine, but afraid of feeling lonely, I wondered if I should I be grateful.

I looked through the woods. Three anglers stood in the clearing on the pool's bank. To me the clearing was a clubhouse without walls. Wondering if I were going to be welcomed, I followed the narrow path into the woods. Soon I stood in the small clearing overlooking Garcia Pool. A bulletin board hung on one of the trees.

The anglers looked at me. They were in their sixties, probably, and were strangers to me. They stood around a small table, a rectangular piece of wood nailed onto a fallen tree. They ate sandwiches, using waxed paper as plates.

I asked, "Anything happening?"

"With all the cold weather fishing has been real slow," the angler with long, hippie-like, gray hair said.

The stocky, bald angler stared at my galoshes.

I said, "They make funny noises when I walk."

"I'm Jim," the stocky angler said. "Where'd you come from?"

"The city. I took the train up."

"I'm Gil," the long-haired angler said.

"I'm Pat," the tall angler said.

"I'm Randy."

"Have you ever fished up here?" Gil asked.

"Two years ago I fished here a lot."

"What happened to last year?" Jim asked.

Thinking the question a bit too intrusive, I answered, "I'm still not sure. Are the big browns still around?"

Jim bit into his roast beef sandwich. "The state," he said with a full mouth, "and the city—your city—aren't taking care of the river the way they should."

"And doing nothing to stop the poachers," Gil insisted. "Guys are coming in, using worms and taking fish. We call the DEP Police, but they take their time getting here, and by then the poachers are gone."

I looked at Pat. He said nothing. He was the quiet one, I assumed.

Jim and Gil filed more complaints in my mind. Soon, however, their words shucked their anger and hatched into cherished stories about big fish they had caught or lost, and about how, ten years ago, the Croton was a great river to fish.

I wondered, *Was there a golden age of fly fishing the Croton the way there was a golden age of fly fishing the Beaverkill? And are these obscure Croton anglers—Gil, Jim, Pat—reflections of the historical Beaverkill anglers, Hewitt, LaBranche, Darbee.*

"After that one got away," Jim said. "I never used 8X tippet again."

Jim looked warmly into my eyes, telling me, without speaking, I was accepted into the club, in spite of my galoshes.

I asked, "Who is Garcia?"

Gil grinned. He chomped on his sandwich like a wolf and said, "He's a heck of a guy and an angler who used to be like the mayor here. Just before he moved to Vermont we named the pool in his honor."

"But we might rename it," Jim said.

"We shouldn't," Gil stated. Looking right at me, he said, "You want to know about Garcia? I'll tell you. Garcia always boasted of his skill at playing and landing fish. Well, one day he forgot to bring leaders; so he borrowed a 5X, fluorocarbon leader from his buddy Sal, and then tied on a Woolly Bugger. About twenty minutes later Garcia hooked a monster brown. He played the fish for about five minutes, but just as he was about to land him, the fish broke off. Garcia lunged with his net, but slipped and fell face-first into the river. His hat came off and started floating downstream. Garcia jumped up and started chasing his hat. Finally he landed it with his net. He put it on. Water dripped down his face. He stared at Sal and yelled, 'Are you sure that was 5X fluorocarbon?' Sal swore it was and said, 'At least you landed your hat.'

"Anyway, about a year later Garcia and Sal were eating breakfast in a diner when Garcia started reminiscing and laughing about his losing the brown and falling into the river. Sal finally admitted that he had mistakenly given Garcia a 7X nylon leader. Garcia yelled, 'You're the reason I lost that big brown.' He jumped up, marched out of the diner and didn't talk to Sal for a month."

The members of the club laughed; so I did too.

"What about the time Garcia spent days trying to catch the big rainbow living below the bridge" Jim said. "He tried twenty different flies; then one day as he ate lunch, an angler no one had ever seen before made three casts under the bridge and hooked the rainbow. Garcia spit out his soda and screamed, 'He took my fish! He took my fish!'"

To me the Garcia stories didn't ring true, but again I laughed; and in my eyes Gil and Jim stood in a warmer light, maybe because I often wrote half-true fishing stories, and because I knew Gil and Jim were just trying to turn someone they missed into a living legend.

Will anyone ever want to turn me into a legend? Probably not. I guess we can't all be Garcias. I remembered I had a seven-seventeen train to catch and that time was speeding by. I asked, "What's been taking fish lately?"

"Nymphs and caddisflies," Gil said. "I'm going with a Hare's Ear. I'll take the water close to the bridge, if that's okay."

"I'll take the middle of the pool," Jim said. "I'm staying with my beetle."

I looked at Pat.

He just stared at the river's mouth.

One by one the members of the club stepped down the bank and waded to their positions.

I thought of walking upstream and leaving the walls of the club, but then I decided I didn't want to be alone yet. *Where can I fit in? All the pool is taken. How about the run, just upstream of the mouth?*

There wasn't a hatch, so I tied on my favorite attractor, an Adams, and waded into the run.

The water was almost up to my knees. It was as clear as cleaned glass. I counted the lace eyes of my boot and then looked upstream. The river, shaded by overhanging branches, reminded me of a train tunnel. The roof of the river tunnel, however, had holes in it. Sunlight poured through the holes and seemed to turn into curtain woven from mist, but when the sunlight crashed onto the river it seemed to break, and scatter, and transform into small, bobbing flames.

I stared at the fire and was sort of hypnotized. *If only I could transform myself as easily as the sunlight can. Maybe then I'll finally put all my character defects behind me. If only. If only ...*

I snapped out of my trance and pulled line off my reel, and cast my fly down and across.

I fished for about an hour, often watching the members of the club and hearing their voices. Most of their words, unfortunately, were washed out by the rumbling water of the turbulent tail. I managed, however, to hear words about Gil's ex-wife moving to, or living in, Vegas.

For some reason, maybe my own projection, I sensed that Gil still missed her. I thought of a woman I still missed. For the hundredth time I asked myself if I had made a mistake when, after she lied and wouldn't apologize, I said good-bye. Then for the hundredth time, I reminded myself not to regret the past. *Besides, I'm not here to find an answer. I'm here to fish!*

Slowly, five steps at a time, I waded and fished upstream, losing sight of Gil, then Jim, then Pat. The sound of the rumbling tail faded into the sound of boiling water.

No takes. I retrieved my line, looked at my cherished Adams and told myself not to be stubborn. I tied on a beetle.

Ten minutes later I landed a twelve-inch rainbow. I pulled the beetle out of his mouth and looked into his eyes. I saw fear, whether it was visible or not, and I wished I could tell the rainbow we were in a no-kill zone.

And if we weren't would I still let him go? Was I as he was: a predator? Or was I as he saw me: a mountain-size monster? An alien? I'm none of those. Maybe I can change the rainbow's point of view. Gently, I put him back into the river and let him go. He darted away, grateful to be free, I was sure.

I cast to the seam behind a fallen tree. My loop was tight. My fly turned over and fell gently; and in my mind I saw orange and gold autumn leaves falling, then winter snowflakes. *Soon it will be too cold to fish, unless I can do away with winter. But I can't, so instead of trying I can use the season to study fly fishing. And maybe, finally, I'll become a good angler. But why? Just to catch a fish and to let him go? What's the sense of it all? Why is it the older I get the more I fish, the less I work? Just who am I these days? Do I know, really?*

The fast-moving water bowed my line downstream and dragged my fly. I had forgotten to mend. I retrieved line and cast upstream. Most of the small flames, I noticed, had gone out. The sun had retreated behind the king-size trees that lined the river and reminded me of a fortress wall. The darkening riffles reminded me of miniature, undulating hills or sand dunes.

The riffles will hide me from the trout. I'll be invisible to them. Thankful, I looked downstream and saw a rise, then another. I thought of wading back, but then a young girl and a man I assumed was her father waded into the river, near the rises.

Now it's too late to wade back, the way it's too late to wade back in life—to play baseball instead of football, a sport I was too small for, and be the athlete my father wanted; and it's also too late to accept my mother before she got sick and to be the close son she wanted.

Downstream, the father stood behind his daughter and moved her casting arm back and forth. Finally, the father let go of his daughter's arm. Her loops widened into circles. She giggled.

Am I ever going to be a father? Or has too much time cruelly passed me by? How can I not regret the past? Can time really be cruel?

I retrieved my line, waded to the bank and climbed up to the path. I walked upstream, toward Frustration, a long, slow pool that, unlike most of the Croton, was lined with short bushes instead of tall trees, and therefore didn't have a roof to block out the overhead sun.

An angler wearing a white baseball hat fished the pool. Disappointed because he was fishing where I wanted to, I watched him false cast. His loops were wide, like the girl's. His line splashed onto the water. He too was a novice angler. I wanted to help him, but knew I shouldn't unless he asked.

I climbed down the bank and waded into the run below the pool. I cast upstream. My beetle landed in the fast tail water. Quickly, I retrieved my line. *Is the water too foamy for trout to see a floating insect? Should I try a weighted streamer? Is that what more experienced anglers would do? How I wish I had a longer, richer angling past to draw from, to predict the future from. But does the past always answer the questions about the future? If so, why don't I know if I'll one day earn enough money from writing to support a son or a daughter?*

Suddenly, I felt powerless and frightened, like the trout I had let go. I cut off my beetle and went with a weighted Woolly Bugger. I cast to the tail, again and again.

Still no takes. *Damn it!* I climbed up the bank and walked upstream.

The novice angler looked at me. He was young, and big, and built like a weight lifter. I smiled and asked, "How's it going?"

"I'm new at this."

"Today that's how I feel."

27

He grinned. "I fish up here because I'm scared that the guys down there will laugh at my casting."

A big guy like you, scared?

"I watched you," he said. "Your casts look so beautiful." He hung his head, shamefully I thought.

Is he just too afraid to ask for help? I said, "I didn't laugh at you. My loops were once wide too."

"Why?"

I smiled. "Well, what I learned is not to pull and push my elbow. Instead, I keep my elbow closer to my body, and rotate my hips and let them move my elbow back and forth."

His dark eyes opened wide. He was really listening, I knew.

Though I didn't have any line out, I simulated a cast and said, "Also, casting a fly rod is different than throwing a baseball. When casting I always try not to lower my hand or the rod tip. To do that, I break my wrist only halfway at the end of my forward cast, as if I'm hammering a nail. On my back cast I don't break my wrist at all."

"Let me try."

"Lift the line slowly off the water. Let the water tension load the rod."

Keeping his elbow in place, he slowly executed his back cast. Again his loop was tight. When it unrolled he cast the rod forward, without lowering the rod tip. His loop was again tight. I was gratified.

He smiled. "Thanks. Where'd you learn to cast?"

"I guess from all over."

His mouth opened. My answer confused him, it seemed, but not having time to explain it, I marched on.

He yelled out, "My name is Brad."

I looked back, told him my name and said, "Maybe I'll see you on the way back."

And maybe I am a good teacher, like the father downstream.

I crossed the bridge on Croton Falls Road, walked past the little island and then the wide, slow bend. I waded into the football-field-long dry-fly pool below the dam and opened my fly box. Staring at about fifty flies, I didn't know which one to choose. Finally, I settled on an Adams. Thirsty, I started to reach for my water bottle, but then I cupped my hand and drank from the river. The water tasted cool and filtered-clean. Suddenly, it was as if surround-sound speakers had been turned on. Birds chirped, but their notes—some loud, some faint, some clashing—were spattered like paint on a wall. They weren't shaped into anything that resembled a song.

I looked up but saw only one big, black bird. *If I could disappear like a bird in the thick leaves of a tree, I'd catch more trout, I believe.* I closed my eyes. The gurgling river, unlike the birds, played a looped and soothing melody. I didn't move, until I remembered I had a train to catch. I opened my eyes. *Since nature always broadcasts in high-fidelity stereo, why for the past hour have I heard only the lone, incessant voice in my head?* I pulled line off my reel and cast toward the gentle riffles. *Forget about having better luck in other pools. Stay in the moment and in this run.*

Upstream the river was as straight as train tracks. The water poured out of the top of the dam. When it crashed onto the river it shined like white silver and rumbled like the tail of Garcia Pool.

An angler sat on the bank. A low branch covered his face. Startled, I flinched. I waited for the angler to say something.

He didn't.

As fast as I could, I waded upstream, past the angler, whose face I now saw. He was old, close to eighty, probably. I asked, "Did I take your spot?"

"No, I'm resting. Are there a lot of guys downstream?"

"Not too many."

"Up here the fishing isn't as good, but sometimes I have it all to myself."

"So you don't like fishing Garcia Pool?"

"I come here to fish, not to talk," he stated. "Besides, the pool isn't anyone's to name. I started fishing the pool right after I got back from the war. There was no Garcia around then."

The old angler wasn't a member of the club, I now knew. I said, "I see your point."

"I've seen hundreds of faces come and go on this river, hundreds, including yours, now. And I've, I've ..."

I waited for him to continue.

He didn't.

Though I wasn't sure why, I found the old man intriguing. I decided to stop wading and pulled line off my reel. I asked, "Do you fish anywhere else?"

"I fished almost every great river in this country: the Madison, the Ausable, even the winding Snake."

"The Beaverkill?"

"Every real angler around here has fished the Beaverkill. I'm tired of hearing about it and its history. History is a thing of the past, like the water flowing by you."

Not quite sure what he meant, I cast upstream and asked. "What's your favorite river?"

His laugh sounded like a howl. It chilled me like a wind. I remembered there were coyotes in Westchester.

"I have no favorite," he insisted. "Why discriminate? Like people, rivers have their own characteristics, but what kind of angler are you who doesn't know that when you come right down to it, all rivers are a chain of riffles, runs, and pools?"

Are people really like rivers? Are we all just a chain of regrets, hopes and fears? I said, "Maybe you can tell me something I should know: How are rivers born?"

"Will knowing help you catch more fish?" He laughed again.

Maybe he's right. After all, will knowing change this moment and help me put my thoughts and feelings aside? Will it help me assume the shape of this river? Help me become as tall and as wide as I can see and hear? Help me meander through this hilly countryside for the next thousand years?

No, because soon I will grow old and weak and unable to stand here and cast a fly rod, unable to lose myself and, in a sense, become only what I see and hear, the way so many other anglers—Jim, Gil, Pat, Garcia—also have, the way so many anglers one day will. So in this moment am I every one of those anglers? Am I therefore no one? Am I just a tiny, tiny link in the chain of infinity?

But today I didn't have to ride the rails and join the Croton Fishing Club. I must, therefore, be more than just a neutral, passing moment. But what? A chain of choices? A self? So when night—a real link of infinity—comes, and I ride the train home, maybe I won't choose to hear or to see my regrets and my fears. Maybe I'll instead hear and see my dreams and memories of catching trout and of becoming a father. I just wish trout could choose between dreams instead of deep pools, or shallow riffles, or long runs.

But trout aren't city anglers.

My line bowed way downstream. I had forgotten to mend, again.

"Are you fishing or dreaming?" the old angler asked sarcastically.

I insisted, "Both, my friend, both."

I retrieved my line and looked at my watch. It said six-forty. I waded to the bank, climbed out of the river, and thought of asking the old man for his name. I didn't. Instead, I just said goodbye.

I fished the Croton three more times that season. Each time many of the faces and the names of the anglers changed.

And the face of the Croton changed, too. It became lower and slower.

And the hatches changed. They became sulfurs, then tricoes.

And, as I knew they would, the colors of the overhanging leaves changed. They became orange and gold.

And though the holes in the roof of overhanging branches didn't change, one cloudy day the holes let in rain instead of sunlight, and the river became pockmarked with large, splattering drops.

But it wasn't only the Croton, the anglers, the hatches and the leaves that changed. I changed too, though not by having a spiritual awaking (whatever that really was). After all, I still had my regrets and fears, but somehow they became shallower, slower, quieter.

And through it all something didn't change. I still walked the streets and rode the subways, carrying my fly fishing gear, wearing my vest and my galoshes.

And I still received stares.

I was still a city angler.

And something more.

Maybe one day I'll exactly know; but today it's all right if I don't.

GOING BACK AGAIN

They say you can't go back again, but I had tried, and returned to Fire Island, and reminisced with my old friends—Patti, Gerry, Bob, Margaret—about the rented beach house and the great summers we had shared; but before I left the island I spun into a black hole of grief over what I desperately missed, and also over what I didn't: my sister's drug use spinning out of control during her two summers on the island. So when Margaret called and told me she had the beach house to herself, I abruptly told her I wasn't visiting.

"The fishermen are catching some big stripers," she said.

I looked at my nine-weight fly rod. "I've been fishing the Hudson."

"You have the rest of your life to fish the Hudson. It's not going anywhere."

I asked, "Is John, the old fisherman, still on the island?"

"I don't know who old John is."

"I'd love to see him, if he's still alive."

"The beach isn't crowded. You'll have most of the surf to yourself. It's a Monday, remember?"

Four hours later, I stepped onto the Fire Island ferry and saw two or three people I knew. Afraid they would ask me about the last few years of my life, or about my sister, I walked to the front of the boat and stood by myself. The sun hung halfway down the sky. It still burned brighter than fire and hurt my eyes. I put on sunglasses and looked straight ahead. The immense sky overwhelmed the wide plain of sun-reflecting water, and then, like a strong army, the sky halted the plain at the horizon line.

Engines blasted on. The ferry moved slowly away from the dock, sped up and chugged across what, in my mind, suddenly looked like infinite, empty outer space. I saw what appeared to be a distant galaxy. The galaxy, I knew, was Fire Island. I thought, *I've taken this ferry ride a hundred times, and yet this is the first time the bay reminds me of outer space. Is it because it really looks like it? Or is it because, after endless hours of practicing writing, conjuring up images has become easier for me? Or is it because after three years of selling article after article and finally feeling a taste of success, my perspective has changed?*

I wish I knew.

Slowly, more and more of Fire Island seemed to float up from the water and to expand like a balloon. I deciphered green trees and different colored wooden homes. I looked to my side and wished my old friends stood next to me. Sad, I wanted the ferry to turn back, then for some strange reason, I wondered what soldiers thought and felt as they crossed the English Channel to fight on Normandy. Many of them, I assumed, had also wanted their boats to turn back. They had had good reason. Did I?

Grief isn't made from lead or shrapnel. Never has it killed me before.

Fire Island and its trees and homes grew to life size. Like an image frozen in an old photograph, the island looked unchanged.

The ferry bumped gently into the small dock. I grabbed my fly rod and my stripping basket, and walked to Margaret's house. She waited on the porch. Because her father was an angler in Ireland, I knew she'd understand when I said, "I'd like to get some fishing in before sunset."

Quickly I changed, set up my fly rod, and marched down the narrow boardwalk and up a short flight of steps. I stood at the top of the high dune.

A fiery corridor of reflected sunlight blazed at right angles to the advancing, gently breaking waves. The long beach was spotted with only a few clumps of people. Instantly, nature painted over the images in my mind of a fast-moving, automobile-choked, concrete and brick city. I became as calm as the beach. The five years I had been away seemed to have collapsed into five days. *Maybe Einstein is right about time being relative, or maybe a part of me never really left the island.*

I didn't see other anglers. The tide was high. I scanned the beach looking for a big point and found one about fifty yards to the west. Seagulls streaked above the surf. Their piercing squawks made them sound like drunken hooligans cruising for a fight. *Why can't seagulls sing beautifully, like other birds? At least they can circle and dive, and show anglers where bait fish, and possibly stripers, are.*

This time, however, they didn't circle and dive.

Though I didn't have their help, I wasn't discouraged. I marched across the soft, warm sand to the harder, cool surf. I walked to the big point where years before, for perhaps the first time in my life, I had voluntarily surrendered to something much bigger than myself: the infinite beauty all around me, a beauty that made me forget all the pain and disappointment I had been through.

Again I wanted to surrender, maybe because nature was a higher power I could believe in. I put on my stripping basket and then false cast, letting out more and more fly line. Finally, I made my presentation cast and let the line go. My front loop took the shape of an arrowhead. My green Deceiver turned over and landed about eighty feet out, just beyond an incoming wave. Unlike the seagulls, the breaking waves spoke softly. They splashed around my legs and greeted me, one by one. As they slid back out, they tried to pull me with them. I fought their beckoning, stood my ground, and retrieved my line, six inches at a time.

I thought of how all the clichés about fishing—being caressed by nature's beauty and being washed of self and time—were true; and though as a writer I always tried to avoid clichés, now, as I stood in nature's canvas, I was sure no one, especially me, would criticize the clichés in my mind.

Fifteen years before, when I had fished the surf with a seventy-dollar spinning outfit, I had also been sure, sure my will to write would make me famous and therefore grateful. But as the rejection slips piled up, my doubt and bitterness had swelled and battered my self-worth with the fury of storm surf.

For the next fifteen minutes or so, I kept looking down the beach. Though I knew it was a long shot, I hoped to see John walking toward me.

My horse didn't come in. Disappointed, I pulled more line off my reel and told myself I'd try to cast even farther. I bent my knees a little more and reminded myself to fully rotate my hips during the cast.

I did. My Deceiver landed about 90 feet away. I was proud of having spent so many hours studying, practicing, and then writing about, long-distance casting.

Wanting my fly to sink to the bottom, I didn't retrieve. I thought of how unexpectedly I had become a published outdoor writer, especially because a few years before my first article came out I had given up writing. John, I guessed, would be surprised by the turn of events. After all, I knew nothing about fishing when I started seeing him walk along the surf, always alone, always wearing a white, floppy hat, always carrying his old brown surf rod. Then one day, for a reason I'm still not sure of, he walked over to me. "I saw you taking notes the other day," he said. Are you a writer?"

"Aspiring."

He looked away from me and studied the surf.

I wondered if my answer disappointed him. I asked, "Is this a good fishing spot?"

"As good as they get, on this beach, that is."

"So even fishing spots are relative?"

He smiled weakly. "I guess everything is."

From that day on, every time John saw me he shared some

angling know-how, and I saw how much I had to learn, how much I needed help; but John rarely looked into my eyes. I became scared that being an angler might turn me into a loner, like John.

Still, I absorbed everything he said. But, wanting to learn even more, I read books and articles on surf fishing, and one day I told John about a new fishing technique I had learned. He looked into my eyes. I was surprised. "When I was a soldier in the Second World War," he said, "I often told myself that if I survived the war I'd go back to Europe and fish the rivers I had crossed as a young infantryman. Well, as you can see I survived the war, and I did go back. But fishing wasn't like I thought it would be. All I kept seeing were the dead and dying soldiers, some floating face down, their blood spreading like smoke and clouding the rivers an ugly red. I was glad when I got home again, even though I wasn't sure if I'd ever fish again. Randy, I'm glad you searched for and found your angling way."

I wanted to ask John why he had told me his story, but he turned abruptly. As I watched him walk along the surf I thought of his description of spreading blood. Impressed, I wondered if he was a writer, or had ever wanted to be.

The next time I saw John he said hello. I smiled and was about to tell him how, partly thanks to him showing me better ways to catch fish, I started searching for better ways to write. But John walked on, surprisingly, and all I could do was watch his image grow smaller and smaller, then finally disappear.

My fly bounced on the bottom. Like a time machine, it brought me back into the present. I retrieved and looked behind me. The sun retreated behind the dune, and withdrew its bright camouflage, exposing faint stars. Night was only a half-hour or so away. *Don't worry about catching a fish. Enjoy what's in reach: this fishing moment. Sooner or later I'll land a striper. Hasn't fishing also taught me to persevere and to have faith?*

I again looked down the beach. Again I didn't see John.

Something told me I never would. Suddenly I was sad. *Am I going to spin back into grief? I don't have to. Yes, soon I'll see other anglers—Richard the actor, Gus the limo driver—anglers who became long-lasting friends. No, fishing didn't turn John into a loner. Maybe the war or something else did. I'll never know. And that should be okay.*

Grateful I didn't have John's blood-soaked memories, I reeled in my line and cut off my fly. *Yes, fishing, and John, helped teach me how to ask for help and how to become a better writer.*

I wanted to thank John. I thought of walking to his house, but I became frightened of learning he had passed away. This time, however, I didn't try to defuse my fear. In spite of it, I confidently, maybe selfishly, told myself that, because I had found my fishing and writing ways, John, wherever he was in the universe, wouldn't mind if I headed straight back to Margaret and spent as much time as possible reminiscing with an old, good friend.

WHERE RIVERS (AND PEOPLE) CONVERGE

There is a pool where two rivers that many anglers consider the birthplace of American fly fishing, the Beaverkill and the Willowemoc, converge. It is called Junction Pool. It is famous because more angling literature has been written about it than about any other pool; so for many anglers, including myself, it is the first Catskill pool we fish, the first pool where, if we're lucky, we meet other Catskill anglers, like Doc, who left such a lasting impression on me that I later created a character with his name and some of his personality, a character who was like him, without being him.

I often think about Junction Pool and wonder if it's part of the Beaverkill or the Willowemoc, or if it's really a combination of the two. Perhaps, however, the Junction is none of those and instead is a place with an essence, a personality all its own.

After all, I now know it's not just rivers that converge and become something new. It's also people; and so, besides the essence of Junction Pool, I wonder about my own essence. To do so, I often look down the river of my life, to the moment, for example, when I thanked Dave Hughes, an editor, for buying my story. *Finally,* I had thought, *after years of trying, I sold a fishing memoir to a national magazine. Suddenly I don't regret being fifty-one.* I sat in my rocking chair and wondered how I should celebrate. Buy a new fly rod? Take a fishing trip? Then, on my bookshelf, I saw it: the old green fishing lure, a seed, perhaps that later blossomed into my becoming an avid angler and an outdoor writer. The lure was hand-carved and cut in the shape of a fat minnow. The tail was joined to its body by small, rusted 0-rings, so when the minnow was retrieved it wiggled. Its eyes were tiny, silver screws. Its lips were carved lines. The lure's hooks had been re-moved, probably by my grandfather, because Sol, his only son, was too sick to fish and could only play with the lure. Years ago I had put the lure on my bookcase so I would always see it and remember Sol. Somehow, however, as years passed, the lure, like a camouflaged fish, faded into the background of my books and my mind.

I walked across the room, picked up the lure, and blew dust off. I thought back to the day my aunt had telephoned and asked if I wanted anything in my grandmother's apartment.

I answered, "I'll come and take a look." I put on my coat and thought of how, after burying three of her children, including my mother, my grandmother probably welcomed the only visitor who could end her grief: death.

An hour later, I scanned my grandmother's furniture and bric-a-brac. There was nothing I wanted. Then I saw the lure. Sol had had bigger and more expensive toys, so why, I wondered, had my grandmother kept only this one? Was it because she knew that, in Sol's eyes, the lure had symbolized what he could only dream of becoming: a healthy boy who fished, played sports and excelled in school?

A voice inside me said, *Take the lure.* I looked at my aunt and pointed to the lure. "This is all I want."

"That? You're kidding?"

"I'm not."

"The lure always brought back bad memories for me, but I know it was important to Sol and your grandmother. I guess someone should keep it."

As I rode the subway home, I stared at the lure, cradled it my hand as if it were alive, and wondered who had made it and who had given it to Sol. After all, fishing was never popular in Bor-ough Park, Brooklyn. *Is there more of a story to the lure than I know? Should I put hooks on it and see if it really catches fish? No, I can't risk losing it.*

I opened the door to my apartment. Without taking off my jacket, I opened one of my photo albums and turned to a faded, black-and-white photograph of Sol, taken just before he got sick. He's about twelve. He wears shorts and a white shirt. He looks away from the camera and smiles as if everything is right with his world. Sol, after all, is my grandparents' first-born and only son. He is their favorite because he is such a big part of their dream of coming to America, of working hard and then seeing their male children become successful professionals: a doctor, a lawyer, an engineer.

I stared into Sol's eyes. *What if Sol had lived and dreamed of becoming a famous writer, disappointing his parents the way I disappointed mine?*

The next photo is of my mother, Gilda. She looks right into the camera and smiles, also as if everything is right with her world. She is, after all, pretty, very pretty, and people tell her so and flatter her. She isn't therefore jealous of her older brother, Sol. She loves and admires him, and is not concerned when, for no apparent reason, he falls down. But then he falls again and again. Other children laugh and make fun of him. My mother often begs him to get up and show everyone he's all right. He struggles to. The children laugh again. My mother insists they stop. They don't, so one day she curses and chases them. She catches one and punches him. Later, Sol asks, "Why am I falling so much?"

Soon they know. Sol, the doctors say, has muscular dystrophy and will grow weaker and weaker and then die. So as the months pass, my grandmother spends more and more time taking care of Sol. Soon he is confined to a wheelchair. Often my grandmother wheels him outside. He can't sit up straight. Children laugh, and my grandmother tells him to ignore the laughter. He cries and demands to go home. Finally he refuses to sit outside.

My grandmother tells my mother, "You have to take my place and become a mother to your younger sisters."

My mother obeys, but feels neglected and resentful. Her resentment simmers into anger and slowly boils into rage. Soon she wishes, secretly, that Sol would die so she could go back to being a child and having parents who pay attention to her; but when Sol dies her rage doesn't. As the years pass, she lashes out at anyone who seemingly wrongs her, especially me, her first-born son. Is it because it is now my task, passed on from Sol, to become the family's first big success? Is that why I can never live up to her high expectations? Though my mother loves me, she often interrupts me, tells me I'm no good. She beats me with anything she gets her hands on. My arms are often bruised so I always wear long-sleeved shirts. And not once does she apologize.

Unable to understand her rage, I blame myself for it, but it is a blame that I repress, until it rises within me and simmers close to rage. The world seems cruel and godless, like a body-littered, blood-drinking battlefield. I yearn for love, and security, and to be heard. I want to become a famous writer. But, lacking self-worth, I'm arrogant and refuse to ask for help. I don't study the techniques of writing. My stories lead only to hundreds of rejection slips. My inability to communicate leads to broken relationships and to a failed business.

Eventually, I find comfort in something that doesn't require communicating: playing softball. Desperate to become good at it and to erase some of my failures, I ask for help by reading article after article about hitting, throwing and fielding. Before long I feel I'm a good player. Maybe the feeling gives me the self-worth to see myself as I really am: someone who can't have conversations or look people in the eye. Luckily, when I'm thirty-five I accidentally read an article about Dale Carnegie's famous book. A voice inside me says, *Read the book.*

I listen, and in the book's pages I see a new way of relating to people. In me I see a deep, deep wound that I want to medicate and heal.

I begin psychoanalysis and become connected to my feelings.

I enroll in workshops, and read how-to books, and learn techniques of communicating and writing, and later even fishing. Finally, I join a twelve-step program and become connected to a new way of thinking about myself and the world. Slowly, I recover, but all the techniques I've learned cannot teach me how to rewrite the long, broken story of my past, so more than anything I just want to forget it. I barely notice Sol's lure on my bookshelf.

Wishing he had lived, and my mother hadn't raged, I closed the photo album. Soon, I remembered how many young successful people got what they wished for and then spun out of control and turned to alcohol or drugs, and some finally to death. *Perhaps*, I wondered, *I wasn't meant to be an early success.*

Grateful, I looked at the lure and wished I could meet Sol and be his loving nephew. Suddenly, the lure seemed like a symbol of what I could only dream of becoming: a successful man with fond memories of loving parents and a happy childhood. *Yes, this lure is to me what it was to Sol. Maybe this lure in some way spans time and, like the Junction Pool, is a place—though one without shape or form—where Sol and I meet, and converge. Yes, some time ago he became a part of me. If only I could become a part of him, but he is long gone, so I am not Sol the way the Beaverkill is not the Willowemoc. Instead, I am like the Junction Pool. I am created by a convergence. But it's not just rivers and relatives who converge. It's people coming together in Twelve Step rooms and sharing similar stories, and therefore feeling less alone and ashamed, and, in my eyes, becoming successes.*

Yes, there are many stories about Junction Pool, and there are at least two about this lure, including an unfolding story that Sol didn't live to see. It is a story I now want to tell, a story about, in part, how this lure will always be Sol's as well as mine. Never again will I let it fade into the background of my bookshelf and my mind.

OPENING DAY

My computer screen went black. Not expected. The end result: I shelled out a thousand bucks for a new laptop and then spent endless hours talking on the phone with tech support.

My dentist told me I needed oral surgery. Not expected. The end result: I shelled out another thousand dollars and then woke up the next morning with a jaw so swollen it looked like I'd run into a Lennox Lewis right.

I wondered, *Why me? After all, I always say please and thank you. Am I falling into a black hole of unexpected disasters? Will I come out of it? Where? When? The opening day of trout season? Yes. Thankfully, some things in the universe happen as expected. So what if my favorite river, the beautiful Croton, is a hike from the train station and is probably high and fast from all the recent rain? In the scope of things, what right do I have to complain after the unexpected outbreak of World War I or the attacks on 9/11?*

None.

And so on the eve of opening day I followed my ritual of piling all my fly-fishing gear on the floor. The next morning I put on my heaviest long johns, my wool pants and fleece jacket, and headed to Grand Central Station, and followed another part of my fly-fishing ritual: buying a slice of Junior's cheesecake.

On the train, I ate my cake and wondered if I would see Hal, Gil and Pat this season, and if they'd read and liked my memoir about them and the Croton.

About an hour later I got off the train and was slapped by wind. *Will the wind kill my casts and turn out to be another unexpected disas-*

ter? Hoping it wouldn't, I walked through the long parking lot and heard humming. The humming, I knew, was the call of the lower East Branch. I listened and remembered how soothing the river's melody was. Grateful to be in nature's beauty, I wondered why I had never climbed over the wood railing and down the hill to check out the lower stretch of the river. After all, it was close to the train station. Was it because few, if any, anglers fished the stretch and, unlike most anglers, I was afraid of fishing all alone?

Not sure, I walked about a quarter mile to Butlerville Road. Only one car was parked near the small, white bridge. Surprised, I walked a hundred more yards, and then into the deserted clearing on the bank of Garcia Pool, the so-called "Clubhouse."

Where are its members? Discouraged, I guess, by the cold and the high water. Why hasn't the water discouraged me? Am I different from other anglers?

The bare, sky-high trees on both sides of the bank clashed with the six-month old vision of autumn I had saved in the internal drive of my mind: trees decorated with beautiful gold, red and orange leaves. The images of the bare trees, on the other hand, reminded me of images I had seen in photographs of World War I battlefields. I told myself not to worry, that soon the river would be lined with overhanging, sun-tinged leaves.

Is that what Nietzsche means by the Eternal Recurrence? Is opening day, along with doing laundry and working the Twelve Steps, also a part of his theory?

Not sure, I followed the part of my fly-fishing ritual I didn't like: putting on my waders and boots, and setting up my fly rod. Suddenly, the sun came out. *Maybe the Croton is rewarding me for showing up.*

Dividing Garcia Pool was a dense band of shimmering stars— a two-dimensional, miniature galaxy of massless suns. I liked my description. I took out my small pad and wrote it down so if I ever wanted to use it I could upload it into my mind and then into one of my stories. But then I wondered if I was overreaching to find beauty in a world that brought me one unexpected disappointment after another.

I didn't see a hatch. *Will a brown Woolly Bugger work today? If only catching fish were predictable.*

The river was high and fast. Wanting slower water to fish, I followed the narrow path alongside the bank and walked upstream to the run below Frustration Pool. I climbed down the bank and waded in. The water was up to my thigh, surprisingly. I pulled line off my reel. Someone walked along the bank, an old guy wearing a floppy hat and carrying a bamboo rod.

I said, "I remember you. Last year you were sitting on that big fallen tree downstream and fishing."

He smiled. "I'm a lazy angler. At my age I have the right."

"Who am I to argue?"

"You're the writer."

"Guilty. You're Mel."

"Good memory."

"Except when it comes to knock rummy."

"I read your memoir. We talked about it at our Trout Unlimited winter meeting. Some guys said the last thing we need up here are more anglers."

"What about you?"

"I loved your piece, even though you left me out, but I'm not surprised. I never win anything."

"Maybe I'll get you in the next one, if there is a next one."

"If?"

"I never know when or if new ideas will come."

"I once wanted to be a photographer, but I just couldn't see the world in a different light, so instead I became an interpreter, of the law. I'm an attorney."

"Interesting take."

"Thanks. How'd you become a writer?"

"I was having trouble casting a spinning rod, even after reading up on it, so I began experimenting with different techniques, and then I started taking notes so I wouldn't forget what I had learned. Somehow I got the idea to turn my notes into an article. When I published it I never, ever thought it would lead to even a second article, but I guess it did. Where is everyone, or at least the diehards?"

"It's too cold. In my case, how many opening days do I have left?"

And how many do I have? Twenty? Thirty? How many opening days does mankind have? Thousands? Millions? Or will war cut the number short?

I said, "You weren't fishing with a bamboo rod last year."

"I thought, why wait to buy myself a gift? It's a shame, though. I have no one to leave it to. None of my kids fish. They'll probably put my fly rods and reels on eBay."

"How do you like bamboo?"

"I'll tell you after I land a fish. Some anglers say that when it comes to fishing rods bamboo is better than graphite. But with all the latest technology, I'm not sure I see why."

"I never fished bamboo, so I don't know. Where are you heading, below the bridge?"

"Home. The water is too cold and fast for me. I'll see you again, I'm sure."

Sure? I was once sure I had more time with my parents. The only thing predictable about cancer, the doctors told me, was its unpredictability. Is life like cancer? I never thought I'd be where I am in the river of life: a childless, journeyman writer. No wonder I can't stop regretting the past, no matter what the recovery books say.

I watched Mel walk down the bank, and thought of how something I couldn't see or touch—like gravity, perhaps—connected anglers and helped us feel less alone.

I roll cast across stream, mended and retrieved my fly, then again. No take. Time for streamer technique number two: I roll cast, then, using the jerk-strip retrieve I had learned in Kelly Gallop and Bob Linesman's book, I worked my fly downstream.

Stay in the moment. Cover as much water as possible and use several different streamer techniques, one right after another. What if time could learn from streamer fishing and not repeat itself? Would the world be even more unpredictable? Maybe Einstein would know.

Again I cast and jerk-strip retrieved. No take. Time for technique number three: I back cast—right into a branch. I'd forgotten to look behind. A spring-training error. I pulled my fly free, luckily, cast three-quarters downstream, and let the river dead-drift my fly. I moved my fly rod side to side, feeding line through the guides. When my fly was directly below me I pointed my rod tip up and waited. No take, still, so I quickly retrieved and then cast my fly closer to the far bank. I listened to the gurgling river and the singing birds.

Yes, rivers are the music halls of the universe. Maybe the Croton is playing only for me. Maybe the river doesn't want to be alone and has a soul and feelings that it transforms into passionate music.

I waded downstream and started another fishing cycle.

Close to the bank the water was foamy. Illuminated by sunlight, some of the foam looked like floating silver dollars. Alongside them were small eddies that swirled so quickly they looked like spinning tops, or miniature black holes. *If they are black holes, maybe, like black holes in the universe, they'll stop time, at least on the Croton. After all, out here I've lost track of my regrets and resentments. Suddenly, I'm happy. Are rivers—their sounds, their images, their beauty—reflections of some sort of divine, eternal plan that scientists like Kepler, Newton and Einstein spent their lives trying to uncover? Were any of those men fly fishermen?*

Again, I waded downstream. The water was higher and faster, and for a second I felt I was back playing high school football and a blocker was trying to take out my legs. I didn't let him. I planted my wading stick behind me, turned and, one careful step at a time, waded to the bank. I walked downstream and climbed down into Garcia Pool. I waded six steps away from the bank. Already, the water was above my waist.

The river, I noticed, had whittled away more of the bank, exposing more roots and bringing more trees closer to their inevitable fall.

"Any luck?" someone yelled. Standing on the bank was a stocky guy I had never seen before. He had a thick, drooping moustache. He reminded me of a walrus.

"No!"

"It's still too early. What you got on?" His voice was as loud as a horn, and as smooth as thorns.

I told him.

"When I drove up I didn't see another car. How'd you get here?"

"By train."

"You came from Manhattan?" he accused.

"Are you holding it against me?"

"No, guys from all over fish here." He sat on one of the benches made from logs and sucked on a cigarette as if he were smoking a joint.

I asked, "Has there been any more talk of renaming Garcia Pool?"

"Since some stupid writer published a story about the Croton, why the hell would there be?"

"Good. Fishing pools, like planets, should keep their names."

"Are you &#%tting me? Fishing pools are not like planets."

"You never know."

"I know!"

I thought of asking him if he knew Gil, Hal and Pat, but I quickly decided that listening to the flowing river was a lot better than listening to him. I roll cast and tried to pretend he wasn't there, but every time I glanced up I faced a grim reality: him sitting there, watching me, judging me, it seemed.

He's waiting for me to do the hard work, then if I get a take he'll go back to his car and come back wearing his waders and carrying his fly rod. Damn him.

The band of shimmering stars, I noticed, was thinner and weaker. I looked up. The sun was sliding behind the high, steep bank. I zippered up my fleece jacket.

Two guys I didn't know walked into the clubhouse. They wore street clothes.

"Hey! I had a feelin' I'd see you guys here," one of them yelled. "What, are you takin' the day off?" one asked.

"No. I finished the job," the walrus said.

"Don't bull&#%t me!"

And so began a long, loud conversation, mostly about fishing, but always littered with expletives that should have been deleted. Unlike most fly fishers, these guys still had one foot in the gutter. Suddenly, I felt I was fly fishing in a three-dollar-a-shot bar. Their voices and laughter drowned out the river's music and the thoughts in my mind.

Again and again I glared at them, but my eyes couldn't complete the connection. They never looked back.

Finally, I decided my best solution was to fish way upstream. I turned and stepped behind me. A hole! Falling, I desperately clutched my wading stick and tried to balance myself. The water felt like ice. My jacket and shirt were soaked. I jumped up. My expletive wasn't deleted.

"You gotta be careful!" the walrus yelled.

"I'm glad you noticed!" I glared at the Walrus. Our eyes didn't make a connection. I waded out of the river, and then reminded myself that being wet and cold was dangerous. I had to head to the train station.

Furious that my long-awaited opening day had been cut short, I wrung water out of my jacket. The walrus and his friends lowered their voices, finally, but of course they didn't offer any sort of an apology. I marched past them, then out of the woods and down Butlerville Road.

When I reached the parking lot I felt a lot warmer. Here, I saw, the sun wasn't blocked by a high bank. I looked at my watch.

The next train was a half hour away. I had time to climb down the hill and finally check out the lower East Branch.

I climbed over the railing and saw what looked like a path. I followed it. It ran diagonally to the river and brought me to the mouth of a long, slow pool. On top of the river was a path of shimmering stars. *Maybe the stars, like me, left the West Branch and found this water a more welcoming hangout.* The river bottom, I saw, was gravel and easy to wade. I looked at the sun. Spewing rays like a geyser, it would keep me warm for another few hours. My opening day wasn't over, maybe.

I waded into the middle of the river, and cast. The water flowed gently and seemed to massage my legs, and for a second I thought that maybe the East Branch knew about my spill and was making an amend. I laughed and soon lost track of time and of myself.

My line slid to the side. Fish on! The shock of the take jump-started my fly rod. It pulsed with life. I squeezed the rod handle and reeled in line. The trout bolted downstream, pulling line. My reel spun. I let the trout run. He slowed, finally. Wading after him, I reeled in line. Thanks to the slow water, the trout couldn't mount much of a fight. Less than a minute later I landed a twelve-inch rainbow.

Now I was ready to head home.

A half hour later, as I rode on the train, I thought it was strange that two unexpected but connected events—the guys on the bank shooting off their mouths, me taking a spill—had led me to discover a small-scale fishing paradise. I wondered if it all was meant to be, and if a higher power had done for me what I couldn't do for myself.

No, I still can't believe it.

I looked at the window. In it, I saw my see-through reflection and felt lucky to have all my hair. *I'm not quite the same person I was years ago. After so many failures I finally asked for help and learned things. Then, tasting small successes, I looked for and discovered better ways of casting a spinning rod, of writing stories. Maybe soon I'll even learn how to heal my deep hurt and to forgive. Unlike a planet, I'm not moving in an endless circle of eternal recurrences. Unlike neutral time, I'm not moving in a straight, repetitious line. But if not for unexpected events, I wouldn't have changed. Can unpredictability, therefore, be part of harmony, part of a great working order of things?*

I wasn't sure, but a few hours later I walked into my apartment, sat down at my desk, and felt grateful for my new, fast computer that burned CDs, and for the advanced oral surgery that had saved some of my teeth.

MEMORIES OF A CENTRAL PARK ANGLER

How should we measure time? By minutes? Hours? Days? If so, is time nothing more than a string of shapeless, carbon-copy moments, each one exactly like the ones before and after? If not, should we measure time in another way, by man-made events such as wars, friendships, fishing trips? If so, July 1st was the most important day in my life, the day my first book was published.

I wondered how I should spend it. By going to the Morgan Library and seeing the first book ever printed, the Gutenberg Bible? By going back to where my outdoor writing career accidentally began: the 72nd Street Lake in Central Park?

I took my first freshwater spinning rod and some of my lures. Walking to the park, I wondered why it had taken me so long to publish a book. After all, thirty long, long years had passed since I first dreamed of becoming a writer. How cruel, how slow time had seemed when I was in the prison of my failures. Yet on this special day for me, as I looked back, cruel time seemed compressed into one giant yesterday.

I entered the park and walked to the big, flat rock at the mouth of Wagner Cove. The lake, I saw, was cluttered with a small navy of rowboats, mostly commanded by laughing kids. To me, the lake was under an invasion. Disappointed as well as surprised, I remembered it was spring break.

I set up my fishing rod and got into my casting stance. I reminded myself to keep my elbow close to my body and to bend my knees slightly. Slowly, I moved the rod back then accelerated it forward. Abruptly, as if I were hammering a nail, I stopped my cast, sending my top water streaking across the cove and landing about twenty feet short of the far, tree-lined bank.

I thought, *not bad.* I pointed my fishing rod slightly downward, twitched it back and forth, and cranked the reel handle. The chugging lure seemed to write a line of Morse code on the water. I jerked the rod tip and stopped reeling. The lure's head popped up and created expanding rings on the water. The rings took my thoughts back forty years to the hula hoop craze. I started to turn the reel handle but then stopped. *Don't rush, especially today. Let the rings dissipate, then move the lure, the way the magazine articles say I should.*

Finally, the rings blended into the flatness of the water. Again I retrieved, and before long I was lost in the cycle of casting, retrieving, casting, and then I remembered one of the reasons why I had started fishing: Fishing and meeting people on the banks of the lake helped me forget my guilt and my grief over watching my mother slowly, painfully die, and helped me forget my fears of my dead-end future.

I retrieved the lure almost all the way to the rod tip, then bent my knees, reminded myself to fully rotate my body, and again cast. My lure landed just short of the far bank. Pleased, I created and watched the hula hoops on the water and remembered that I had longed to become a great caster who could cast all the way to the far bank of the cove. It didn't happen. Almost always my lure landed at least thirty feet short. Frustrated, I read up on casting and learned a few techniques that helped me cast farther, but still well short of the far bank. I was at another dead end, it seemed. Like a mad scientist, I experimented with my own casting techniques, suspecting, but not fully admitting, that for me, casting, like playing softball, was really about becoming very good at something and erasing, in my mind at least, some of the links in my long line of failures, especially my inability to forgive my mother.

Slowly, very slowly, the experiments worked; and I cast farther and farther, until finally, when the leaves started falling, I cast all the way across the cove and snagged my crank bait on a tree. Thrilled, I thought that, during the long winter, I might forget what I had learned about casting, so I decided that as soon as I got home I would write down my techniques so I could review them in the spring.

As I wrote I thought of other struggling casters, of how my techniques could help them. During the next few days I turned my notes into an article and then sent it off to a local magazine. Six weeks later I still hadn't heard from the magazine. I phoned the editor. He told me he wasn't interested.

Angry, thinking I had racked up yet another failure, I said, "Would you be interested in an article on bass fishing in Central Park?"

"If you could get it to me by May 1st I'd be very interested."

I hung up, put on my coat, marched to a magazine store and bought two fishing magazines. I read several destination articles, then picked out one and used it as template. The next day I wrote my article in three hours. A month later I read my first published words, not thinking they would lead anywhere. Still blind to the long, up-and-down road that lay before me, I baby-stepped my way through writing and publishing one article after another, then, knowing that my mother would be proud of my small successes, I decided to make a big amends to her for all the years I had been unable to forgive. I turned to writing a book.

The hoops on the water had disappeared. I had forgotten to retrieve. I cranked the reel handle and thought, *I didn't become a published writer how and when I wanted to, thankfully, because success, I'm sure, would have steered me away from my journey of recovery. Did I become a writer, therefore, in a Higher Power's time? An accident's time? Or I did become a writer regardless of time?*

I turned from the cove, looked across the lake and scanned the banks for other anglers. I didn't see any. Surprised, I wondered if the anglers had outgrown the lake, or even fishing itself. *Will I one day? How many hours have I spent fishing this lake? How many hours talking to tourists and strangers?*

"Are there really fish in the lake?" The accent was English and thick as grease. It belonged to a man about my age. His shirt was light gray, and his chest was shaped like a barrel. He reminded me of the Tin Man, but a nice camera hung from his neck. I assumed he had a heart.

I answered, "Big bass."

"In England I used to fish for carp."

"Used to?"

"Now I'm more into traveling, but I still have my father's fishing rods. Maybe they're worth some money. How could I find out?"

"You can check on the Internet."

"The Internet? Right. How'd we ever live without it?"

"That's what they said about the wheel."

He laughed. "Good luck."

"Thanks." I cast. *Another future memory, I'm sure. Memories, I guess, are like stars: new ones are always forming. But memories don't have real dimensions. Do memories, therefore, exist only in the expandable hard drives of human minds, like the first memory I have of fishing this lake?*

She wore thick, granny glasses and looked like a middle-aged hippie. She told me she was from Boise. I told her I had never met anyone from Idaho. She told me Boise was a great city with a beautiful river and a great orchestra. I wondered if she was just a bit biased, but wanting to fish instead of talk, I looked away from her and watched my fishing line, but out of the corner of my eye I saw her standing there, watching me. For me, the silence between us became uncomfortable. Finally, she broke it and asked questions about New York. Soon I realized she too was lonely and sort of lost. I looked at her and suggested places in the city she might be interested in seeing.

"I used to fish with my father," she said. "Funny, for so long I kind of forgot how those were the only times I really got to talk to him. I guess now that's he's gone I try to forget that he was only sober for two things: working and fishing."

I thought of asking her if she was a twelve-stepper, but I wasn't sure if asking was appropriate. Wondering what to say, I came up blank, until I remembered what I had read about listening and showing empathy by reflecting back a person's words. I said, "That sounds like it must've been really hard on you."

"It was. That's why I don't think about it, I guess. Did your father take you fishing?"

"My father only took me to do only what he wanted to do."

"Are you from Manhattan?"

"Brooklyn, originally. I went to the same high school as Sandy Koufax."

"Too bad you didn't have his fastball. I'm sorry, I mean about the Dodgers moving."

"My uncle still hasn't gotten over it, even though we got the Mets."

"What was growing up in Brooklyn like?"

"Great. Filled with endless street games: stickball, football, hide-and-seek. I guess back then we all thought the whole world was part of Brooklyn."

We continued talking, mostly about the two cities we loved, and soon talking to her seemed more important than fishing.

She looked at her watch. "I should really get going. It was great talking to you. Maybe New Yorkers really are friendly."

I laughed.

"I'm Joan, by the way."

"I'm Randy." We shook hands and said good-bye. As I watched her walk away I felt grateful I had met her. At first I wasn't sure why, until I realized it was partly because I had helped someone feel welcomed in a huge, foreign city.

I snapped out of my memory and reeled in line. *I hope Joan, wherever she is in the world, has found the love we are all looking for.* I thought back to when I was so shy I couldn't look anyone in the eye or express my thoughts and feelings, to when I finally admitted I needed help, and then took workshops and read books, and learned how to communicate. *If only I hadn't spent so many years unable to ask for help. Yes, I was damaged, but I didn't cause it. Today I must not regret or deny the past. My memories will keep it alive.*

I walked along the south bank, cast, and then scanned the rowboats. Unlike time, they moved in different, random-seeming directions. I scanned the trees that surrounded the lake like a necklace. I scanned the apartment buildings that lined the park like a fortress wall. Suddenly, I felt I was looking from a distance at a giant, three-dimensional photograph. *Yes, I feel so detached from the lake, as if it's a parallel universe. Maybe I've outgrown fishing in Central or maybe, as I watch and hear people talk and laugh, I wish I too were with close friends instead of with memories.*

I thought of Robert, my old fishing friend, and remembered the day we fished the Beaverkill, and I took him to fish the Covered Bridge Pool, one of the most beautiful places on earth. We waded into the river. Ten minutes later I looked upstream. I didn't see Robert. An hour later, when I waded out of the river and walked to the car, I saw him. He was drinking beer. On the back floor of the car were two empty beer cans. It hit me: Robert was a closet alcoholic.

I thought of my friends, Steve, Joe and Bill. Though I had known them since high school, and though they had witnessed my failures, they had never asked to read anything I published.

Suddenly angry, I retrieved my lure. *Yes, I'm taking refuge in resentments that I've turned into recurrent carbon copies of themselves. Why? Is it because I'm scared of critics panning my book? Or is it because I'm scared of facing the impending fork in the road of my life? If only I were more like time and never felt fear or reached forks. But thankfully, I can change directions.*

I reeled in my line and walked along the winding asphalt path to Belvedere Fountain. The large, three-tier fountain was surrounded by a square red-brick plaza. The bricks reminded me of the Yellow Brick Road in the *Wizard of Oz*. I thought of Dorothy trying to escape time, or at least the present, by dreaming up people and places. I thought of myself trying to escape by reliving real memories and then trying, unsuccessfully, to change them.

Who was better off, Dorothy or I?

I walked to the concrete bank, cast and watched my lure fly across the lake. The lure carried me back to the morning of 9/11, to when I stared at the TV in disbelief, feeling I had been beamed down into a surrealistic, terrifying land. I craved familiar ground, a place where I would find a hint of sanity, of comfort.

I grabbed my fishing rod and my lures and meandered to the plaza, but instead of finding sanity and comfort I found obsession. Again and again I wished I could turn back time and erase the horrible carnage of 9/11 and of the world wars, but wishing, I knew, couldn't dent time's armor. After all, time didn't have shape or mass. Even worse, time didn't cry or care.

Who was better off, time or I?

I could never answer, year after year.

I retrieved my lure, slowly, continuously. Instead of hoops or Morse code, the lure carved a short, narrow wake.

A woman and her two dogs walked up to me. The boxer stared at my fishing rod. The bulldog looked at me and smiled as if I were his friend. I petted him.

"We take them fishing all the time in Wisconsin," the woman said. "They know the drill. Every time they see fishing rods they get excited."

I said, "So even dogs have good memories of fishing."

"Absolutely." The woman smiled. "Good luck. Take care."

Yes, maybe it's the people I meet that bring me back to fishing this lake. People, unlike moments in time, aren't interchangeable.

I remembered meeting the woman who told me she was visiting from Canada. I told her, "You don't have a Canadian accent."

"I'm from New York. I moved to Toronto many years ago for a teaching position, but now I'm retired. I love the way the city is taking care of the park, and building a new park along the Hudson River. I wish I could move back."

"Why don't you?"

"I had a rent-controlled apartment I had to give up. Now there's no way I could afford a free-market one in Manhattan."

"What's Toronto like?"

"It's a nice city, but for some reason, it never felt like home."

Feeling sorry for her, I wondered what would happen if I moved to Boise or anywhere else. Would I regret it and always want to move back to New York.

"Maybe," she said, "if I stop coming back to visit I'll forget how much I miss this city." She said good-bye and, though she didn't know it, walked into one of my memories.

I again cast. *Time, are you really a flow that, like the Yellow Brick Road, leads somewhere? Or are you just an infinite cycle that, like the red bricks of the plaza, has no beginning, no end? Time, perhaps you don't really exist at all. But I do have hopes. I do have a past that I've learned from, and I do have thoughts that are my private, toll-free wormhole so I can learn my past and then change and grow.*

"Any luck?" someone asked.

I turned and saw a young couple. They held hands. He carried a tourist map. I said, "Yes, I had some luck."

"What did you catch?"

"Memories."

He laughed.

I smiled and hoped a future memory was about to start.

PIER FISHING (WITH A FLY ROD)

I didn't become a lawyer or a doctor, as my mother wanted, but when I was in my early thirties I did become a surf fisherman on Long Island. Several years later I climbed to the top of the fishing ladder, so to speak, and became the most sophisticated of all anglers: a fly fisher. (When I wear my fly-fishing hat and vest, people tell me I look every bit as much an angler as Brad Pitt does in *A River Runs Through It*.) And so, to feel like I'm really a part of the exclusive fly fishing club, I've read a countless number of fly-fishing books and articles. So what if I don't catch as many fish as I feel I should.

I didn't become the great American novelist, as I wanted, but I did become an outdoor writer. (When I give people my business cards they are impressed.) So what if I've earned an average of $120 an article and still don't have an agent?

I didn't become, back then, a lot of things, good and bad, including a pier fisherman. Piers were magnets for anglers on the lowest fishing rung: bait fishermen. Besides, what self-respecting fly fisher wants to fish, standing on concrete or wood, with a railing in front of him?

One, maybe, who's often too tired to travel up to the beautiful Westchester trout streams, and who is therefore willing to accept the challenge of saltwater fly fishing. (How could I not with my hometown, Manhattan, bordered by two routes of migrating striped bass: the East and Hudson Rivers?)

But I had a problem: I didn't have a fly rod that was heavy enough to land a striped bass or a blue fish. My solution: spend over $600 for a top-of-the-line one. Wasn't I worth it, in spite of my shortcomings? My therapist and co-members of my twelve-step program would say so. Unless they suspected I was trying to mask something. What? Grief and self-blame over the loss of a fishing friendship? But how often had Robert kept me waiting in subway or train stations? Too many times to count. How often had he read my published articles or stories? Not once. And when we did fish together how often did he insist on leaving early, probably so he could have a drink? Always. And did he ever apologize? Never.

For whatever the reason, I reached deep into my pocket and shelled out $625 for a new fly rod.

Now, where to fish? In Long Island City, Queens, I had heard, was a new fishing pier. I took my fly-fishing gear, paid a $2.25 subway fare, and checked the pier out. It was shaped like a gigantic capital T. The bottom leg of the T was about thirty yards long and six yards wide. Guarding its south side like twelve-foot soldiers was a row of tall wood pilings. Casting and retrieving between them would be a chore. The top of the T, shaped like a big rectangle, was a watering hole for five bait fishermen. The fishermen wore baseball caps, dungarees and old jackets. Angling attire? Not exactly. Real anglers wear waders and fly fishing vests or fanny packs. About ten spinning rods leaned on the north railing.

The mile-wide East River vaguely resembled a trout stream. Downstream, on the far bank, instead of a meadow was a long, low building, the United Nations' Assembly. Upstream, instead of trees there were tall and short, wide and thin, stone and glass buildings. From my new Queens perspective, the skyline looked as if it were cut from a giant cookie cutter. It didn't seem intimidating, unlike the bait fishermen whom I suspected wouldn't even say hello to me.

I decided not to fish near them.

I set up my fly rod, tied on a deceiver, and put on my stripping basket. The bait fishermen, I saw, watched me as if I were from Mars, or even Pluto. One laughed, at my official fly fishing hat, I guessed. Another reeled in his line, stuck a chunk of bait on his hook, and cast. He stopped his surf rod way too low. It unloaded like a slinky, lobbing the lead sinker, at most, 50 feet.

I thought, *Bait fishermen don't even know the basics of casting. Casting and retrieving are too much work for them. But did I come to the pier to dwell on other people's casting defects, or on the damn railing in front of me? No.*

I false cast, shooting more and more line between two pilings. Abruptly, I stopped the rod. A tight loop shot across the water. My fly turned over and splashed down about 90 feet away. *That will show the bait fisherman I know a thing or two about fishing.* I retrieved, faster and faster, but I was no match for the current. It swept my line under the pier and embedded my fly in a piling. Four dollars gone on only my first cast, or so I thought. A fisherman with blond, hippie-long hair marched down the pier with a long gaff and freed my fly. I retrieved all of my line and yelled, "Thanks!"

"You're welcome."

Realizing I had to cast and retrieve against the current, I turned around and cast upstream, but a gust of wind took my line and smashed it into one of the pilings. Embarrassed, I didn't look at the bait fishermen. I retrieved my line and walked past the pilings to the top of the T. The upstream railing was entirely occupied by a small legion of bait fishermen, each one armed with not one, but several spinning rods.

The chutzpah! The injustice! After all, I'm one angler, so I take up one space and play by fair rules. But complain? To whom? The mayor? The only violations he cares about are the ones he can ticket and raise revenue from. Well, some bait fisherman take undersized fish. But look at their cheap fishing rods, some with broken tips. They can't afford anything better. Maybe they're not exactly little Frankenstein monsters.

I decided not to squeeze between them and force them to make room. I faced Manhattan and cast as far as I could.

"Wow!" one of the fishermen shouted.

Feeling respected for a change, I twitched and retrieved my fly as it swung downstream. Instead of hearing the murmur of a trout stream and the songs of birds, I heard loud Spanish chatter. I tried to tune it out. I couldn't. *Solitude means nothing to them. Well, at least no one is shouting into a cell phone, yet.*

I heard the names of baseball players, so I assumed the bait fisherman were arguing about the Mets and Yankees. I sided with the Mets, as always.

A big downstream bow formed in my line. I wondered if I would be able to set the hook if I got a strike. My fly swung directly below me, finally. I moved the rod tip up and down. No strike. I retrieved line, six inches at a time.

What's the challenge, the skill of casting bait and then waiting for a strike? Why not just buy fish in a store? I don't understand bait fishermen. They're like Einstein's theories to me.

Feeling I was light years ahead of them, I wondered if I should have called Robert. *But risk a long wait? Not again. Stay in the moment, not in my bait fishermen resentments. Lose myself in the urban, but still beautiful, outdoors.*

Again I cast. My line floated over seams, riffles, eddies, and smooth-as-glass water, what all looked to me like miniature mountain ridges and desert plains. The shapes held firm, as if they respected each other's turf, and as if the entire East River rolled on wheels.

"What you fisheen'?" The accent was from the Barrio. It belonged to a fisherman wearing a faded Mets cap. He walked toward me. He was about sixty years old and needed a shave.

"A Clouser."

He stared at my fly rod and seemed to see gold. Somehow he knew a good fly rod when he saw one.

I asked, "How's the fishing here?"

"So-so."

Was he discouraging me from coming back?

"If you wanna to catch fish," he said, "use bait. Wanna worm?"

"I only use flies. Is there a bathroom around here?"

He pointed to a small building on the near bank. "Dhere."

How convenient, especially because I'm not wearing waders.

"God made our little fisheen' world so pretty," he said. "I try to come here every day, except Sundays."

"Why not on Sundays?"

"I go to church."

I thought of how I had issues with God. The East River, I saw, seemed to transform reflected sunlight into diamonds. Suddenly, the river looked as beautiful as any trout stream or Gothic cathedral.

"Good luck," he said. He walked back to his friends. The one wearing the Yankee hat opened a white cooler, took out a can of beer and held it up. He looked at me and smiled.

I said, "No thanks." I took out a cigar and lit it. Two of the bait fishermen nodded. They approved. *Would they if they knew I was smoking a $1.25 knock-off? Probably. Bless them.*

During the next two hours the bait fishermen and I often exchanged glances. None of us caught a fish. The East river slowed and erased the seams and eddies like a teacher erasing chalk from a blackboard. *Maybe slack tide is the river's way of meditating and coming to terms with itself and the rest of the world, especially with invading anglers? Shouldn't I also have slack time? Tomorrow I'll meditate.*

I looked at my watch and saw go-to-work time. I reeled in my line.

The fisherman wearing the Mets hat walked toward me. "Sunset is dhe best time. Sometimes I fish spoons. I work dhem deep down for stripers and higher up for blues."

So he knows something about real fishing. "I'm going for stripers so I probably should have used a sinking line."

"Next time I'll show you how I fish spoons," he said.

Was he inviting me back?

I walked back to the subway. *The bait fishermen were probably born into poverty. Who am I to judge them? When I go back to the pier, maybe I'll wear my Mets hat. Even though I didn't catch a striper, I had a good time, probably because I began to feel connected to the bait fishermen.*

I decided, however, that the next time I went fishing, instead of dealing with finding room on a pier railing, I'd wade into water, somewhere, and have all the room I want.

A week later, I rode the train up to Mamaroneck and walked through the town to Harbor Park. The big harbor was shaped like a tilted, upside-down pear. The top of the giant pear—the part of the harbor closest to me—was full of small sail and fishing boats. Dividing the pear in half were two rows of red buoys. The bottom of the pear had a small opening that spilled into Long Island Sound. The pear motif was reflected on the far bank, in the shape of trees with short trunks and big round tops. Ripened by autumn, these trees had long, gold-colored leaves. Breaking up the pear motif like riffles breaking up the surface of a flowing stream, were taller, cone-shaped trees that had reddish-orange leaves.

I set up my fly rod, put on my waders, climbed down the bank and waded toward the buoys. A narrow wooden pier slowly came into view. The pier, I soon saw, was about a hundred feet long. Four bait fishermen, each with one rod, fished from the pier, leaving plenty of room for any angler who wanted it.

I didn't. I felt comforted by the harbor water—water, unlike a trout stream, I didn't have to read. The buoys read it for me. They mapped a narrow channel that striped bass used like highways. I cast toward the channel and retrieved, again and again. Often I looked at the pier, watched the bait fishermen and tried to decipher their distant chatter.

Yes, I'm in a gem of the vast earth, but with no one to share it with. But fly fishing is supposed to be about solitude and nature.

Then why has meeting anglers been so important to me? Should I wade back to the shore and fish off the pier?

No! Today I'll try to enjoy solitude.

An hour later I hooked my first striped bass, a schoolie. With my 9-weight rod, I didn't experience much of a fight, but at least I was on the scoreboard, so to speak. Now I can give into my fatigue, and my loneliness, and head home.

I promised myself to return to the harbor as soon as I could, but two weeks later the forecast predicted a chance of rain. Rain, I told myself, wasn't going to stop me. After all, no matter how much I wanted to, I couldn't turn over and restart the hourglass of the striped bass migratory run. *But maybe the big stripers don't swim all the way into the back of the harbor. Maybe I'll be better off fishing from the pier.*

The pier was deserted when I got there. The thick, gray blanket of clouds had scared away the bait fishermen, it seemed. Hard-core anglers they obviously weren't. Across the harbor the long, drooping, half-bare branches were now sprinkled with sand-colored leaves, their final shade before being shed by time.

I set up my fly rod, cast just past the channel, then retrieved. Dead leaves floated by in a huge, birdlike formation. *Did the leaves fall simultaneously from the same tree? In nature is death often timed, like a football game?*

The outgoing ripples, I noticed, flowed faster than the leaves. *Maybe the leaves are in no rush to leave the harbor, to drift into the great big sound and disintegrate into nothingness. But leaves knowing they were on a death march? Then why, especially after my mother's death, didn't I know I was on one too, and that reconciliation often runs out of precious time?*

An angler walked by, carrying a small bucket and what I knew was a quality spinning rod and reel. He wore a white GORE-TEX jacket. He set up a Carolina rig with what looked like a dead minnow. He cast, stopping the rod abruptly and slinging the minnow way past the channel. He swept the rod tip to the side, then, reeling in line, pointed the rod back to straight ahead, then to the side. He repeated his Carolina retrieve.

Maybe some bait fishermen really know how to fish.

Again I cast.

"I never saw anyone reach the channel with a fly rod," he said. He leaned his spinning rod against the railing and walked to me. He inspected my fly rod, but didn't seem to see gold.

"Are you a fly-casting instructor?" His accent was slight Castilian, I guessed. I thought of asking if he had read *Don Quixote*, my favorite book, but I wasn't sure if pier fishing and literature mixed.

I said, "Just a person who spent four years mostly practicing long-distance casting instead of fishing."

"Why'd you do that?"

"I'm obsessive. Besides, writing casting articles was a great way of getting published." *And erasing my failures and repairing my self-esteem.*

He asked if I tied flies. I said I didn't have the time. Winter, he said, was his time to tie, and to invent new patterns.

I asked, "So why are you fishing with bait?"

"After using flies most of the season and giving the stripers a real chance, I deserve some easy strikes."

Unlike Don Quixote, or me, he seemed at peace, at least with his angling world.

I told him about my line bowing on East River and asked, "Will I be able to set the hook?"

"Use the tension between the line and water to help. If the bow, let's say, is moving to the left, move your right foot back. Then if you feel a strike, quickly rotate your hips, and sweep the rod all the way around to the right, and pull down hard on the line."

I introduced myself. His name was Carlos. For the next hour or so we talked about the waters we fished. We shared a love for the Beaverkill and the Croton. My loneliness burned away, and then sunlight warmed my face. The blanket of clouds was splitting in half and, surprisingly, reminded me of Moses parting the Red Sea. Suddenly Carlos coming out of nowhere and answering one of my biggest fishing questions seemed like a small miracle. *Is he an angling angel? After all, he's wearing white. But I thought I didn't believe in angels or in a loving higher power.*

A few hours later, as I sat on the train, I wondered if Carlos and I should have exchanged phone numbers. *But will friendship, like the rising sun, reveal his defects? Are we anglers better off meeting and then going our own ways?*

I still wondered when I fished piers in Brooklyn and on Roosevelt Island, still wondered when Thanksgiving passed and New York was blessed with a mild weekday. Robert called and insisted he wanted to go fishing. I told him to meet me on the 69th Street Pier. He said he would.

The football-field-long pier wasn't crowded, thankfully. At midfield two bait fishermen leaned four rods on the railing.

I asked, "Que pasa?"

"Nada," one answered, smiling. "Fly fisheeng? Wow! Good luck."

"Gracias." I walked to the end of the pier, remembering the church-going bait fisherman who had told me he fished spoons on different levels. I tied on a Clouser and cast straight across, toward New Jersey. I let my Clouser sink. My line bowed downstream. Something told me Carlos also was fishing on this mild day.

An hour later, high tide became slack tide. Robert still hadn't showed, but it didn't matter. The strangers I talked to kept me company.

I walked to the north side of the pier, tied on a popper, and cast upstream. My new strategy didn't pay off. Were two schoolies all I had to show for my $625 fly rod?

The sun looked like the eye of a giant Cyclops peeking over

New Jersey. But the sun's face, like the face of Mr. Potato Man, was made up of many parts, including what seemed like the mouth of a fire-spewing dragon. The sun beamed down a burning path across the Hudson River. When the sun set, I knew, it would also set on my fishing year. Slowly, the Hudson darkened into gray, but instead of letting go of all its light, the river seemed to divide the light and reshape it into flickering columns. The columns, I saw, were not reflections of moonlight but reflections of the Riverside Park, man-made lights. To me, the reflections looked like the linear-shaped galaxies of a contracted, upside-down world—then the reflections looked more like giant, vibrating subatomic strings, particles supposedly holding the key to understanding the universe and the possibility of even a twelfth dimension. *Am I in it?*

No, just in a place where a person's disappointments, such as losing a friend, take up a single speck of space: in the three dimensions of a pier.

Five miles upstream, the lights of the George Washington Bridge formed the shape of a huge, hanging smile. The smile, surrounded by the shapeless, dark-blue sky, didn't have a face. *Is the smile the mouth of the Cyclops? If so, it's certainly a happy monster, maybe even a bait fisherman who won't eat the Manhattan skyline. Are the monster's nose, chin and ears also disguised and hidden in the beauty surrounding me and surrounding all the piers I fish? Beauty, perhaps like the idea of a God or a Higher Power, doesn't have boundaries like rivers and harbors. Beauty can spread, even to monsters.*

A voice inside me said it was time to let go of fishing for the year, and to make peace with winter. I retrieved my popper in a straight line, frequently pausing and creating rings on the water. The movement, I realized, reflected my fishing adventures. They too moved in a line of time, frequently creating fishing rings filled with anglers, including bait fishermen, I could speak to and then feel less alone.

Yes, it's time to forgive lower-rung bait anglers, the way I'm learning to forgive myself for not being all I once wanted to be. Isn't this awareness what I really have to show for my $625 fly rod? So even though Robert won't be the friend I want, I will remember that I too can have boundaries, and that I can wait for him on my terms: not in a train station, but in a stream or on a pier. And even if I travel alone, I'll feel grateful for angling adventures that, like a beautiful river, will flow on and on.

THE GIFT MY FATHER LEFT BEHIND

Many stories have been written about fathers or grandfathers passing down their favorite fly rods or reels. I wish I too could write such a story, but my father never fished a day in his life. In fact, as I look around my apartment I don't see anything of his. My father was not the kind of person who gave his children gifts or sent them cards, even on our birthdays; but that was less than the half of it. After my parents divorced, my father never paid child support, even though he helped his girlfriend, Mary, buy a house so her children would have a place to live. And yet in spite of all his shortcomings—and yes, all my resentments toward him—in the endless, flowing monologue of my mind, I often now see something important he left behind.

I'll tell the story about it this way:

I wondered if I should even look. Reluctantly, I walked down the long row of recliners. I saw it: a tan, lean one that matched my furniture. I sat in it, rocked, and felt as if I were sitting on shaped air. I was as comforted as when I fished a beautiful trout stream. I thought, *Don't even think of spending money on this recliner. But I'm so comfortable, and this chair would be good for my slack time, good for meditating.*

I closed my eyes and thought back to when, to escape my mother's yelling and screaming, I lived with my father, a man who often interrupted me and told me I was wrong. One day he brought home a gift from his client: a beautiful, padded, antique rocker. He put the rocker in the living room, facing the sliding glass doors, overlooking the rectangular harbor of Sheepshead

Bay. I sat down and rocked in rhythm, I soon noticed, with the small, rocking boats.

On the water a long path of late-afternoon sunlight divided the harbor into almost perfect halves. The path was orange, a much brighter shade than the orange streaks in the sky. Covering the path like gravel were small, flickering stars. The stars and the boats bobbed in rhythm. On the other side of the harbor an American flag fluttered violently while a row of bare trees vibrated gently. Though I didn't hear music, I imagined that the flag and the trees were a small orchestra playing counter-melodies.

For the next hour or so I watched the harbor as if I were watching a compelling movie, but this one had no characters, no sequence of events, just moments that seemed to repeat themselves in an endless circle that had somehow shed any hint of monotony. But the movie's story, I noticed, did unfold: The water darkened into gray. Suddenly, one of the ends of the orange path disappeared, as if it had sunk. Then more and more of the path sank, like a big ship, and seemed to pull the orange streaks out of the sky, and pull the anger toward my mother and the imperfect world out of me.

I put on rock music and watched the water and the sky slowly darken to black. As they did, the stars that seemed to sink reappeared, almost magically, in the sky. They beamed brighter and brighter.

Day after day I sat in the rocker, not knowing that my growing love of watching the shimmering water would, years later, lead to my love of standing in a riffled, gurgling stream and casting a fly rod.

I came home from school and the rocker wasn't there. Stunned, I asked my father, "Where's the rocker?"

"I gave it to Mary. She needed a chair for her living room."

"That was my rocker! You had no right to take it from me!"

"Everything bothers you," he scolded. "I'll get you a new one."

It was another lie, I knew. My feelings froze, the way they had when my mother raged and cut my beautiful Wilson baseball glove in half. A second winter settled inside me. It lingered, seemingly to tell me yet again I wasn't entitled to anything good, like the comfort and security of a loving home.

I never again mentioned the rocker to my father. I tried to wash it from my mind.

Two years later I graduated from college and moved into my own apartment. One day my father telephoned and asked me to meet him. Curious, I drove to Manhattan. My father took me to a showroom crammed with wooden rocking chairs. I was surprised.

"Pick one," he said.

I picked a wooden, antique-looking one. I could barely, however, bring myself to thank my father.

An hour later I put the rocker in my small apartment, put on music and sat down. I was comforted, for about twenty minutes, until the rocker's hard seat and back felt uncomfortable. So during the next few years I bought a thick cushion and a footstool. Still the rocker was uncomfortable, but for thirty years I wouldn't allow myself to get rid of the only gift, the only amends, my father had given me. Besides, deep down inside me it was still winter. My feelings of entitlement, especially for a comfortable rocker, were still frozen over.

Fast forward to many years later. I returned from a fishing trip to the Beaverkill River. Feeling soothed by the images and sounds of the river, I had begun to feel that maybe everything was all right in the world. My sister had left a message on my answering machine. My father was very sick. Shocked, I flew to Miami and walked into his hospital room. He smiled and greeted me as if he didn't have advanced colon cancer. He picked up the remote control and put on the Met game.

I said, "You don't watch baseball."

"You do."

"Well, not so much anymore."

"You used to love the Mets."

I remembered how he had never wanted to take me to a baseball game, and had always dragged me to see movies only he wanted to see. *Yes, by putting on the Mets he's making an amends. I wish it hadn't come so late, but I'll surely accept it.*

I wondered how, in this day and age, a grown, educated man had failed to take care of himself, had never had a colonoscopy. I was angry, not just because he should have known that my sister desperately needed a parent—even an imperfect one—but also because, in spite of everything, I wanted him to have time left to enjoy his life, to enjoy living on his sailboat, arguing on internet discussion boards, and, yes, smoking pot.

"How was your fishing trip?" he asked.

"Fishing trips are always good."

"Boy, I never thought you'd become an angler. We were a football family. Besides, we're from Brooklyn."

I laughed. "I guess I was too small for the NFL."

"I wish I could go back and take you to play Little League baseball instead of football. A few years ago Walter told me he watched you play softball on Fire Island."

"Maybe there's a reason that time flows only downstream. If I had played baseball and become really good, maybe I'd still be holding on to an unfulfilled dream, and maybe I'd still be playing ball instead of fishing. Then, I wouldn't be a published writer."

My father smiled, and in his expression I heard the words, "Thank you."

I said, "I guess one of the beauties of fishing is that you don't have to be big or fast or even good at it to really love it."

"How much does a real good fly rod cost?" he asked.

"About six hundred dollars."

"Really?"

"Yes. So much research and development goes into a six-hundred-dollar rod. To me, they're works of science and art."

"Then they're probably worth it. I never saw any sense in fishing, but right now, I'd give the world to be able to become an angler. I'm glad that you have."

Suddenly, in my mind, I drifted upstream, into the future, and saw my father sitting outside with me, listening to me, approving of me, especially the part of me that was a writer.

My vision didn't materialize. My father died a few days later.

I flew home, sat in the rocker he had bought for me, and thought that it would take awhile for the grief to sink in. Suddenly, I cried. Grief had found me as if it knew exactly where to look. Because I didn't have a family of my own, I felt like an orphan, an orphan trying to hold on to the few precious possessions of his past, like the rocker.

Three months later, during low tide of my grief, I turned on my TV and watched the Mets. For a few moments I dreamed that I was part of the team, and then I looked downstream in the river of my life. I saw myself when I was thirteen. I was in a sporting goods store with my father. I looked at rows and rows of baseball gloves. I picked out one that cost twenty-seven dollars, the amount I had saved by working for my father as a laborer in his small construction company. On the top row I saw a more expensive glove, a Wilson. The sales clerk took it down and handed it to me. The soft leather molded to my hand. The glove felt like a part of me. My expression must've shown love because my father told me that sometimes it pays to get what you really want. He reached into his pocket and gave me some money. During the next few years I often oiled and even slept with my cherished love. But after my mother cut it in half, I forgot my father's words and didn't buy anything good for myself, until many years later when I sold my first fly-fishing memoir and, reluctantly, bought a top-of-the-line fly rod.

Still, I didn't feel I deserved it, so I fished most of the long trout season without believing the beautiful rod was really mine.

I opened my eyes, and my mind as well as my body was back in the department store. I looked at the recliner's price tag: three hundred dollars, on sale. In my mind I saw the antique rocker, then my beautiful Wilson baseball glove. *Yes, in my father's eyes I was entitled to have the glove and other good things. Yes, my father gave me something more important than a rocker or a fly rod. He gave me a glimmer of self-esteem, an early first step in the way of soothing the pain inside me.*

I stood up, walked to the salesman and said, "I'll take the chair."

A few minutes later I walked out of the store, and thought of how my father never gave me the love or approval I wanted. Suddenly, I wished we had fished together. In my mind I looked upstream in the river of life in front of me. I said, "Dad, thanks for the gift you did leave behind."

AN ANGLING LEGEND OF THE HARLEM MEER

Once, not that long ago it still seems, I was an unpublished writer. Then I wrote a fishing article and sold it. After a long, surprising run of publishing in magazines, and after a wild sprint of writing a book, my dream drifted downstream of me. I didn't pick it up. You see, I no longer wanted to endure endless hours, staring at a computer screen, revising sentences about ten times, and I no longer wanted to endure submitting up to twenty times, and then only occasionally landing, like an elusive brown trout, an acceptance. Besides, didn't I finally deserve to enjoy endless hours doing what I loved, what ironically my writing had kept me from: fishing?

Yes! This striper season I wouldn't miss, especially with so many new piers sticking out of Manhattan like the legs of a giant caterpillar; so on an October morning I checked the tides. High tide was six hours away. Another disappointment, though small in the scope of things, I reminded myself, especially when I had another fly-fishing option: the Harlem Meer.

An hour later I walked into Central Park. The Meer, at least the half I could see, looked more beautiful than I remembered, perhaps because the autumn leaves were orange, yellow, amber, and different shades of green. Again it seemed unfair that leaves looked most beautiful just before they fell.

The wind chilled me. I zippered up my fleece jacket and looked for anglers. I saw only one, near the ice-skating rink.

I set up my fly rod and walked along the bank. Suddenly the Meer's shape reminded me of a giant boomerang. Maybe the shape wasn't an accident. Maybe whoever designed the Meer wanted to remind people that the Meer's beauty was never going away.

I liked the image of a boomerang, so habit told me to take out my pad and write it down. I listened, but the more I looked at the Meer, the more its shape reminded me of a bird with long, outstretched wings. Again I wrote, then I thought that migrating birds, like boomerangs, always came back, and that the two images, therefore, were connected by a sort of bridge I couldn't see or touch.

The angler near the ice-skating rink was an African-American, about my age. With his old, beat-up spinning rod and reel, he reminded me of the bait fishermen I often saw on piers. He flipped a jig and landed it gently a few inches from the small island.

Impressed, I said, "I haven't been here for a while. How's the fishing been?"

He glanced at me and then studied my fly rod. I hoped he didn't know the cost of a GLX.

"I don't remember you. Did you give up fishin', or just give it up here?"

I wondered, *Is he accusing me? Interrogating me, to see if I now felt too good to fish the Meer? If so, when it comes to fishing, I have nothing to atone for.*

I said, "I've been busy with work."

Without looking at me, he worked his jig up and down.

A silence. I didn't like it, or him. I walked on.

"Wait a minute," he said. He reached into his beat-up canvas bag, took out a small photo album, and showed me pictures of several big bass he and some of the other Meer anglers had caught. He looked into my eyes, sadly I thought. "Those TV anglers got nothin' on us," he stated. "I'd like to see them fish from a bank, without fish finders and all those rigged rods. Let's see how many fish they catch then."

"Not many, I bet."

He grinned.

I asked, "Do you know Thomas and Kenny?"

"The old guys? Sure. I just saw Thomas in the small cove. He's fishin' from a wheelchair. He's got cancer. He told me Kenny's cancer came back. They're legends here. Fishin' here won't be the same without them."

"No it won't. I'm Randy." I held out my hand.

He shook it and smiled. "My name is Bruce. Nice meetin' you. Nice fly rod."

I walked to the start of the sharp bend and put on my stripping basket. *Bruce, like the bait fishermen, was probably dealt a bad hand. I shouldn't judge his bitterness, especially when I often wish I was someone else in this card game of life: a lawyer, a father, a person with close friends who actually read some of his published articles or stories.*

I false cast, letting out more and more line. I landed my popper well short of the island. I cursed, but then forgave myself for making a bad cast. I looked across the Meer. Boys threw stones into the water. Angry, I wanted to yell and tell them they might hurt some fish. Luckily, I didn't have to. They ran out of the park, taking my anger with them. Suddenly, in my cleaned-out mind, I saw a long dock, an image I'd seen in a new edition of George M. L. La Branche's classic book, *The Dry Fly and Fast Water*. I retrieved my popper, six inches at a time, and thought it was sad that so few New Yorkers knew that some of the first American fly-casting tournaments had been held at the Meer, and that La Branche and the great fly-rod builder, H. L. Leonard, had competed. *There should be a bronze plaque, insuring that the legacy of the tournaments won't be washed away. At least La Branche is remembered for his book. Will I be remembered for mine? How I hope so.*

I cast again and again. No strikes. I turned away from the small island and faced Fifth Avenue. Casting lefty, I landed my fly in the deeper water.

Ten minutes later, still no luck. I walked around the bend, into the cove that, to me, was shaped like a bird's head. At the back of the cove Thomas sat in a motorized wheelchair. I thought it was sad that Thomas had gone from using a walking cane to a wheelchair. He false cast about twenty feet of line and then landed his fly in the middle of the cove. I stepped toward him, but realized he might want to be alone with his thoughts and his memories. I didn't take another step. Wanting to respect his fishing water, I cast across the mouth of the cove and remembered that Thomas, a former corrections officer, had once told me he regretted spending much of his life locked up with, as he called them, "the dregs of society."

Yes, he too has a real right to be bitter.

I heard the sound of a motor. Thomas was riding toward me. He stopped about ten feet away.

"I remember you," he said.

"It must be my fly-fishing hat. No hard feelings if you laugh at it."

"Kenny gave me your story about the Croton."

"I'm glad someone I told about it managed to read it."

"It was really wonderful and different, but you don't look old enough to come to terms with a mid-life crisis."

"I guess I'm still working on it."

"Speak louder, please. I'm having radiation treatments. They told me my lung cancer is… is…" Thomas roll cast.

I waited for him to finish his sentence. He didn't. I reeled in my line and walked over to him. Because my mother had passed away from lung cancer, I thought I would be able to come up with words that would comfort him. I couldn't. Again I felt like a writing failure. I put my hand on Thomas's shoulder and said, "I'm sorry. I wish I knew what to say."

He smiled. "There's nothing you can say. I just got to love the little time the man upstairs has left me. I just wish a fishing season was starting instead of ending. Well, at least I'll have fly tying to keep me busy. Do you tie?"

"Now that I'm finished with writing, maybe I should learn."

"Finished with writing?"

"My well is dry, so to speak. I too want to enjoy the fishing time left to me." *What a stupid thing to say. Thomas would give anything to have half the time I have left on this earth.* "Thomas, I thought of you last week. I took the court officer exam."

"My niece took the test too. I hope you get the job."

I had never heard him talk about his children, so I assumed he, like me, didn't have any. *Will he die alone?* The thought scared the daylights out of me, I guess because I was scared I would too.

"Thomas, I didn't take the correction officer exam, thanks to what you had said."

"Where would I be without the city's great medical plan and great pension? Twenty years ago I retired with what seemed like an eternity to fish."

I was surprised by Thomas's newfound gratitude. *Will I have to wait for terminal cancer to remove my character defects?*

The sun, I noticed, had slid behind the trees, stealing my precious fishing time. I looked into Thomas's eyes. They pulled me like warm magnets. I decided to shuffle my day's fishing time and to play my new hand by listening to Thomas.

I asked, "What are you fishing with?"

"Pheasant Tail nymph. Crappie love them."

A flock of screeching seagulls landed on the water.

"Thomas, since when do seagulls come here? Do you think they lost their way?"

Thomas smiled. "Seagulls aren't like people. They came from the East or Hudson Rivers, knowing people will feed them and they won't have to work for a living."

"Like they're on welfare."

"Exactly."

"I'd like to also think they came because the Meer is so beautiful. Look: baby geese. It's amazing how instinct tells them to swim in straight lines, behind their parents."

"Yes, it is. So many generations of geese and ducks, I've seen.

My mother's cousin, Eddy, first took me fishing here when I was about ten. We fished with cheap bamboo rods for bluegills. Eddy was the real quiet type. The only thing he talked to me about was sports, especially about how much he hated the Yankees. He wouldn't even tell me where he lived. But I suppose just being with Eddy, especially outdoors, made me feel like I was as good as other boys whose fathers hadn't died."

Thomas looked over my shoulder, breathed deeply, then looked back at me and continued, "When I got older Eddy bought me a spinning rod and taught me how to fish for bass. I still remember when I caught my first one, right near the steps over there. Fighting a big bass was nothing like fighting a bluegill. I guess that's when I got really hooked on fishing. Then one day, after Eddy said good-bye, I followed him, hoping to see where he lived. But he saw me and shook his fist, and seemed to turn into a monster with flame-throwing eyes. 'Don't you ever spy on me again!' he yelled.

"Scared he might hit me, I ran away and cursed myself for doing wrong, especially when day after day I waited for Eddy to take me fishing again. He never did. Finally, I asked my mother why Eddy didn't want me to see where he lived.

"'Maybe because he enlisted in the Army, and knew that because of this damn war, he might not see you again.' My mother cried.

"To make a long story short, about a year later I came home and found my mother crying. She looked at me and said, 'Thomas I've got something to tell you. Eddy was killed somewhere in France. How could a man like Hitler come to power? I'll never understand. But what I do understand, as clearly as two plus two equals four, is that one day you'll find out the truth, so it's only right that you find it out from me. Eddy isn't my cousin. He was the only man I ever loved. He was married to someone else. Eddy… Eddy is your father.'

"What did I feel? Randy, I felt numb, as if I were shot full of

Novocain, but as the days and weeks rolled on, I began to hate Eddy and my mother's lie. Over the years my hate got smaller and smaller, but I couldn't leave it behind—until I met so many inmates who had never known a real, or even a fake, father. Soon I remembered that before I hated Eddy, my father, I loved him. And so I became thankful my father had given me something, fishing, that I've loved my whole life. Suddenly I wanted to love him again, and I did. I suppose that's why, even though I've fished all the great waters of the Northeast—the Beaverkill, the Salmon, Martha's Vineyard—the Harlem Meer is the water I always come home to. Often I see my father in the water's reflection, smiling like a boy. Often I see him on the bank, teaching me how to cast a spinning rod. That's when, for moments at least, it seems as if all my yesterdays merged and re-formed into this one big today."

Now it was my turn to feel shot full of Novocain. I remembered the power of a good story, especially told by someone who had never written one. I remembered how my father, in his way, had also deserted me and how, even after his death, a part of me wanted him back, partly because I knew if he read my memoirs he would be proud, very proud.

I didn't have to wonder why Thomas told me his story. He wanted me to write it and, in a sense, keep him alive in the small world of fishing. But did I, a little-known writer with a long line of mistakes in life, have power over who lived and died? If so, did I want it?

The wind, I noticed, had retreated. The leaves were still, and the Meer looked like a life-size frame on a movie screen. Then I realized it was a three-dimensional frame, seemingly a moment frozen in time. Did the Meer somehow create the frame to acknowledge Thomas and to give him a little more precious time? If so, I wished the much larger world could do the same, for him and for other cancer patients as well.

Though the water had become darker, the colors of its vibrating reflections—trees and tall buildings—had brightened, ironically.

Again I wish that, as the sun sets on our lives, we became beautiful, like autumn leaves. Are men and women less deserving than leaves because of our mistakes, especially our long, long string of wars? But now, as I look back, I see my cancer-stricken mother having been more beautiful just before she died.

A flock of geese dived and shattered the calm surface of the Meer. The geese and seagulls soon formed two distinct camps on the water. The camps reminded me of opposing armies on the night before they clashed. But the geese swam away. The seagulls didn't pursue. *Yes, geese and seagulls are more like anglers sharing the same lake or river than like opposing armies fighting, killing for the same land.*

"Randy, I have to go. Good luck with your test."

"Thanks, Thomas, thanks."

I watched him drive out of the park. *Will I see him again? If I don't, I'll miss him. How I wish I could see my parents again. But at least I can still see my sister. Thank God she never overdosed. I wonder what's going through Thomas's mind, knowing he might not ever again see the Meer? What will his final journey—to where time cannot go—be like? And what will my final journey be like? Is it better if I don't know?*

I looked up. The full moon hung right between the two tall, matching buildings, and reminded me of a football flying through goal posts.

I cast toward the back of bird's head. For the next twenty minutes or so I covered most of the cove's water, still without luck. Wind chilled me. Time on the Meer flowed again. To keep my false casts from being blown out of shape, I cast harder, but in the advancing darkness I couldn't see my casts unroll. My popper landed in the back of my vest. I pulled it out and was about to cut it off and head home when I noticed flickering in the park lamps. They were coming on. *Are these man-made inventions, like judges handing out justice, giving me back the fishing time I gave to Thomas? Maybe the Harlem Meer, unlike the wide world, is governed by its own laws of fairness.*

Standing still, I watched the lamps burn brighter and brighter. They reminded me of stars in the dark sky, and in my mind the Meer changed from a giant boomerang or flying bird to a small part of a beautiful, miniature galaxy.

Again I false cast, but the man-made light was short-ranged and didn't reach my rolling fly line.

Yes, seeing my line unroll in the darkness is really a metaphor for my now seeing that what's important isn't what the crazy world owes me, but what I owe the world: more stories that might help people come to terms with the unpredictable, often disappointing game of life.

Suddenly I felt like an angler who's fought and landed several good fish: grateful for another day of angling and ready, very ready, to go home. I reeled in my line, cut off my popper and took my fly rod apart. I retraced my steps along the bank. Again I looked up. Except for the real stars, the sky had turned pure black, but something told me the sun hadn't set on my writing, that I had at least one more story to tell, one about Thomas.

I felt lucky, very lucky, to be a writer again.

NOT SO GREAT ANGLERS

What makes a great angler? Don't ask my friend Robert. An aimless, failed actor, he's clueless that a great angler is obsessed with learning and experimenting with fly-fishing techniques, and is obsessed with overcoming fishing obstacles and disappointment.

Often I see those great anglers on rivers. They spend time reading the water before making their first cast. Then they often change flies and leaders, and sometimes fish tandem rigs. Also, they often write notes on what flies and tactics took trout.

Robert was a world away from being a great angler. I was an ocean away. You see, I read a fair amount about fly-fishing techniques, but, unlike great anglers, I didn't measure success by the number of trout I caught. I measured success—if you can call it that—by how much I enjoyed being in the midst of a beautiful river or surf, by how much I enjoyed meeting other anglers. So instead of always changing flies and leaders, I often tied on a streamer and covered as much water as possible.

And yet in one way I was like those great anglers. I too was obsessed, but with writing and with long-distance fly casting. For years I spent countless hours studying writing and experimenting with fly-casting techniques until, pleased with my progress, I finally decided to put my writing and casting obsessions behind me, and to devote much of my time to enjoying fishing.

It didn't happen. Soon I realized why: I was bored with streamer and dry fly fishing. I needed a new challenge. Quickly, I found one: to become a great nymph angler. To do so I bought Charles Brooks' classic book, *Nymph Fishing for Larger Trout*. I read each chapter and, like a college student, I highlighted the essential ideas and techniques.

According to Brooks, there are over ten different methods for nymph fishing. Of the ten, he felt the Brooks Method was the most productive. To fish the method he used a sinking line, a short leader and a heavy fly, like a stonefly. Next, he waded into a fast, rocky pool, cast upstream and let the fly sink to the bottom. Finally, as the fly drifted downstream, he followed it with the rod tip.

The method seemed easy enough. I decided to try it, especially because I thought I knew the perfect pool for it: Waterfall Pool on the Titicus River. The Titicus was only about a half-mile long and, in most places, about twenty-five feet wide. Trees lined both banks. Their overhanging branches formed a leafy, mosaic-looking roof. But the roof had gaps in it, letting in different-shaped beams of light that crashed on the water, shattered, and turned into small, one-dimensional, flat flames. I wondered why such long beams could so radically, so quickly transform themselves while I had to struggle year after year to transform myself and overcome my defects.

I hiked upstream. As usual on the Titicus, I didn't see another angler. I had the eerie feeling I was alone in the world. I didn't like it. I reached Waterfall Pool. It was filled with pockets and seams. Carefully, I waded in and took cover behind a large boulder. I pulled line off my reel and cast my fly upstream, just below the foamy water. Holding my fly rod parallel to the water, I followed my drifting fly. A downstream bow formed in the line, the way Brooks said it would. Suddenly, the fly stopped drifting. Was I hooked up on the bottom? I pointed my rod tip up. I wasn't hooked up.

Again I cast and followed my drifting fly. Again it stopped. Frustrated, I wondered why. Then I decided to try the Brooks method about ten feet downstream.

I got the same result, again and again. My frustration condensed into anger, almost as instantly as the long beams condensed into flat flames. I wondered, How did I manage to mess up the techniques I read only yesterday?

Not having fun, I came up with an excuse to change to a streamer and not feel like a quitter: There was no point in fishing the Brooks method until I reread his chapter and learned what I had done wrong.

I waded out of the river and hiked downstream to the Big Bend. Though the bend looked promising, most of the times I fished it—always casting a dry or a streamer across stream—I got skunked. This time, however, I felt I had to erase my nymph fishing failure. I decided to fish my tried-and-true method, a method so simple, I never told anglers it was my favorite: dead-drifting a Woolly Bugger straight downstream in broken water.

I tied on a size 12 and waded into the river, just upstream of the bend. Moving my fly rod side to side, I fed line through the guides. The current pulled my fly downstream, just below the low, overhanging branch. I raised the rod tip up, waited, and then retrieved about six inches of line.

A take! I swung my rod up and pulled down on the line. The rainbow jumped. He wasn't very big, but landing him would put me on the board, so to speak. Desperately, I wanted him.

I got him. I let the trout go. *Maybe I'm not such a bad angler after all.*

And so I soon lost myself in the back-and-forth of dead drifting and retrieving. Though my nymph fishing failure still muddied—in my mind, at least—the beauty all around me, I suddenly heard a chorus of birds and the steady counter-rhythm of the gurgling river. *Yes, I'm enjoying being alone. Another take! Now I'm beginning to roll!*

The second rainbow was a little bigger than the first. I released him and then waded downstream, step by step. Methodically casting and retrieving, I covered much of the bend.

Bang! The take jolted me like electricity. My fly rod overloaded from a power surge. It throbbed and bent into the shape of a giant crowbar. I felt as if I were trying to pull a cinder block. The trout wouldn't budge. *It must be a brown.* My tug-of-war was a stalemate. Wading downstream, I reeled in slack line and tried to get below the trout. He waded downstream with me.

Remembering what I had read in Kelly Gallup and Bob Linseman's book, I applied steady pressure and tried to lift his head out of the water. I couldn't. *He must be a monster! He'll tire before I do. As long as I keep him out of the fast tail, time is on my side, unless he breaks my 5X tippet.*

I pulled my elbows and arms close to my body. My fly rod still throbbed. It seemed to pump electricity and the trout's will to live through me. *Why didn't I use a 3X leader?*

The trout yanked the line. My reel spun, but only for a few moments. The throbbing eased. Again I tried to lift his head. Again I couldn't. *Will this stalemate ever end?*

I held my fly rod still, letting it absorb all of the trout's will. *He's weakening, finally!*

I lifted his head. He was a brown. *It's now or never. Please tippet, don't break.* Slowly I reeled. The brown was about twelve feet away, then eight, then four. *He's bigger than any trout I ever caught. A monster! Don't pull too much of him out of the water and let him rotate and break off.*

Back and forth he swam. I kneeled down, put my hand under the trout and grabbed him, finally. *I won! I'm redeemed. Thank God for streamers!*

"Don't worry, Mr. Monster. We all deserve to live." I held the big brown under water and then let him go. He darted downstream. I caught my breath. My heart, however, seemed to beat harder than before. After winning a big fight I wanted one more.

I didn't get it. Then the dusk thickened. Fearing darkness, I headed home.

On the train, I thought of how, after spending so much time studying nymph fishing, I'd caught the biggest trout of my life on a simple streamer technique. Was that ironic? I kept asking myself the question until I walked through my door, dropped my fly-fishing gear on the floor, and reread the chapter on the Brooks method. I didn't get an answer to why my stonefly had stopped drifting, so I went online and posted the question on a fly-fishing bulletin board. A week later I still didn't have an answer. Maybe becoming a great angler was going to be harder than I thought.

My cell phone rang. Robert's number was on the screen. Suddenly, in my mind was the memory of when he had caught a huge bass in Central Park and, instead of releasing it, he had taken it up the main road and looked for someone to take and then send him a picture. By the time he had released the bass it was nearly dead. *Should I answer the call? He did have a bout with early prostate cancer.*

I answered. Robert asked if I had been fishing. I told him about the monster trout I caught.

Robert third-degreed me about where and how I had caught the trout. I answered his questions, one by one.

"So you just used a Woolly Bugger?" he asked, as if he didn't believe me.

"Do you want to swear me in?"

Robert didn't laugh. He, I knew, wanted to go to the Big Bend and repeat my tactics. As always, he was looking for an easy way to catch a big trout.

"When are you going up there again?" he asked.

"Next Monday."

"Can I go with you?"

Will he show up late again? I said, "If you want, meet me on the 11:48."

During the next few days I continued wondering why my stonefly hadn't drifted downstream. Finally, it hit me: Because some of the boulders were so big, the stonefly couldn't drift over them. The answer was so simple I wondered why I hadn't thought of it.

But what nymph fishing method would work in water littered with boulders?

Again I opened Brooks' book and read. The best method to fish Waterfall Pool, it seemed, was the Rising-to-the-Surface method. I looked forward to Monday.

Robert showed up only five minutes late, after I started eating my slice of Junior's cheesecake.

"It's so good to go fishing with you again," Robert said. We got on the train, and he asked for a summary of my fishing season, often interrupting me to learn exactly where and how I had caught fish. Annoyed, I was glad when we finally got off the train and walked to the river. I took a Woolly Bugger from out my fly box. "Robert, tie this on."

He did. I tied on a caddis nymph. We hiked to the Big Bend. I described my dead-drifting method, wished Robert luck, and walked to Waterfall Pool. I waded in, pulled line off the reel, cast slightly upstream and let the nymph sink. I pulled slack out of the line and slowly raised my rod tip, then lowered it and simultaneously retrieved line. Again and again I recycled the technique until the caddis was about a foot from the rod tip. No take. I waded a few steps downstream and started a new cycle. A take! But the trout was close to me, so I landed him without much of a fight. My studying had paid a cheap dividend.

About an hour later I won my second short fight. I released the rainbow and decided to see how Robert was doing. I strolled downstream. *Maybe I'm finally on the road to becoming a great angler.*

Robert was sitting on the bank.

I yelled, "How'd you do?"

"Great! Look."

I walked up to him. The monster brown—I assumed it was the same fish I had caught—lay at his feet.

"Too bad you didn't bring your camera," Robert said.

"Why didn't you release him!"

"A beauty like that? I want a picture."

"I didn't tell you how to catch him so you could kill him."

"It's legal on this river—I think."

"I don't care if it is."

"When we get back to the city you can get your camera and we can go to Riverside Park. With the right background no one will know where we are."

"I'm not taking any pictures or ever again telling you how to catch a fish." I marched downstream.

"Wait for me."

I glanced over my shoulder. Robert put the monster brown into a plastic bag, then into his backpack.

I reached the long, narrow Bridge Pool and tied on a streamer. Robert walked past me and told me he was going to fish the slow water below the bridge. Not answering, I waded into the narrow run just upstream of the pool. I dead drifted my streamer downstream, but instead of seeing the beauty all around me, I saw the monster trout lying at Robert's feet. Then I saw him finally releasing the near-dead Central Park bass.

I didn't like the images, but I couldn't flush them from my mind the way some of my recovery literature said I should. My fishing day had turned sharply, like the Big Bend, but for the worse. I decided to go home without Robert.

He called me that night. I didn't answer. He left a message asking why I had left without him, and then had the chutzpah to ask me to call him the next time I went trout fishing. I didn't, even though I often went back to the Titicus and the Croton and often experimented with new nymph fishing techniques. As the end of the trout season neared, I caught more and more fish, but because I usually hooked them close to me, I had mostly fast one-round, low-voltage fights. And often, so often, I hooked my nymph on the river bottom and had to wade in fast, rocky water to free the nymph. Sometimes, however, I got so disgusted I just broke the nymph off.

In spite of my short fights and river-bottom hookups, as winter set in I bought more books on nymph fishing, but the more I read, the more the techniques seemed to merge into each other. I couldn't tell where one ended and another began, and then the confusion started throbbing in my head. Instead of aspirin, I gave myself slack and stopped reading. My mind felt free. *Should I close the book on trying to become a great angler?*

During the next few months I kept wondering.

I checked my voice mail. "Randy, it's me, Robert. Guess what? My prostate cancer came back, but the doctors say it's nothing they can't handle. They increased my antidepressants. I'd certainly love some company."

I called Robert and told him I would stop by that night. Wanting to get him a get-well present, I went to Orvis and scanned rows of books that could help Robert become a better angler. Abruptly, I turned my back on the books and bought him a new fly box.

He smiled like a boy when he saw it. His apartment was the way I remembered it: messy, and as if furnished from the Salvation Army: an old table and a couch and chair that didn't match. Piles and piles of newspapers were everywhere.

How can he live this way?

The framed photograph of Robert holding the monster Titicus trout jolted me like a violent take.

"My neighbor took the picture for me," Robert said.

"I can hardly tell that's the Hudson River behind you. I like the blurred background. And the spots on the trout are as sharp as a razor."

"Being that I'm spending so much time home and trying not to feel scared—well, I just can't help staring at the picture. It reminds me that I really love fishing, and that I really want to put this cancer thing behind me. That was some heck of a fight that trout gave me, but sometimes—maybe because now I often think of death—I think I should have let him go. I hope we soon go fishing together."

"We will. I promise."

"Will you have a beer with me?" Robert asked.

"Sure."

We ordered in Italian food, and as we ate with plastic forks and knives, we recalled, one by one, some of our old fishing adventures, like the time we went striped-bass fishing and, within a half-hour, bluefish bit off three of my five-dollar poppers. As we reminisced, the adventures became, in my mind at least, as vivid as a movie on a screen. Neither of us mentioned Robert looking for someone to photograph the big, Central Park bass.

Yes, in spite of my differences with Robert, I'm enjoying being with him.

We watched a hockey game. When it ended I said good-bye. A few minutes later, as I rode uptown on a bus, I stared at a wide avenue that seemed to flow downstream of me, and I thought it was sad that Robert, at his age, was so insecure he relied on photos of fish he had caught to feel good about himself. Maybe, I realized, it was his insecurity that had led him to become a depressed alcoholic. Suddenly, I was glad I had helped Robert catch the monster trout. Though I still looked out the bus window, in my mind I saw myself struggling at nymph fishing and feeling frustrated and angry.

Maybe Robert's easy-way-out approach to fishing is as good as anyone's. Why was I so unfair, so self-righteous that I expected him to live up to my standards? Is it because I'm also insecure and still can't accept myself? Is that why I want to become a great angler?

Yes, the answers, like dead drifting a streamer, were simple, but not easy, I knew. I hoped they wouldn't drift by without a take—my take—and that in the years upstream of me, I'd stop trying to change the defects in people and in the world, and instead I'd see more good than bad. *Yes, if I can do that I'll have a real spiritual awakening.*

The next day I went to Orvis and bought an equal number of streamers and nymphs.

FISHING BENEATH A MARBLE SKY

I felt a chapter of my life was drifting to a close. Yes, I had gotten so much out of fishing: a way to come to terms with my past and my grief, and a way to live my dream of being an often-published writer. But dreams, even if they become real, aren't made of physical substance like flesh and bones, or even made of filmed images or recorded sound. Dreams have a shelf life and, because of the flames of time, burn themselves out and evaporate. So in the end, dreams are more like merging rivers than like morning mist: Dreams, instead of disappearing, flow into something new.

And so I now dreamed of earning more money, a lot more, and of finally building a retirement nest-egg. After years as a limo driver, I dreamed of rejoining most of the human race, and having my nights and weekends free so I could watch important sporting events, and so I could take adult education classes and meet new people.

And again I dreamed of starting a family.

Is it any wonder that when I saw in a newspaper that New York State was giving the employment exam for Court Officer Trainees, my new dreams hardened and seemed to have the weight of bars of gold?

I took the test, along with about 10,000 others. Six months later I got my results: I had done well, very well, and was informed I would be called for a preliminary physical.

I had the job, I was sure.

A few months later I look my physical. Afterwards the nurse said, "You failed the vision test."

"Failed? How did that happen?"

"It wasn't because you didn't study. Your eyes need correcting, a lot of it."

"I beg your pardon."

"It's nothing to apologize for."

"I'm sorry—I mean, I thought wearing contact lenses was okay."

"To be a court officer you have to meet certain requirements, without glasses or contacts."

"But I did so well on the written test."

"Our rules are firm."

Sarcastically, I said, "Written in stone, I guess."

"I'm sorry."

The white ceiling, the yellow walls, and my hopes seemed to be closing in on me. I jumped up and left the office.

Outside, I thought, *I was so sure I had the job, the way, years ago, I was so sure I'd become a famous writer. Sometimes I feel like I'm cursed.*

During the rest of the long, long day and the next morning, I felt as if I was being pulled into a rip tide of grief. I was afraid of drowning. *Don't panic. Swim out of it. Use techniques of recovery as a higher power and remind myself I didn't cause the state's requirements. What I can do is go fishing.*

I took my fly-fishing equipment, rode the Path train to Hoboken, and walked to the long, wide concrete pier. Covering most of the pier was a big lawn, creating the impression of a small park. Parallel to the pier, about two hundred feet downriver, was the old Lackawana ferry terminal. The side of the terminal was getting a facelift, but not for the better, in my opinion. The new face was flat and white, emptied of the flowing baroque-like ornamentation of the old green facade.

I looked up. The thick, gray clouds seemed to form a high ceiling, reminding me of the inside of a huge marble building. The forecast wasn't for rain, so the clouds didn't seem ominous.

The Hudson River was calm and murky and reminded me of a deserted asphalt highway.

Because of the cloud ceiling, I guessed the stripers, if they were around, would be close to the surface. I decided to fish a popper on a floating, shooting-head line. I put my fly rod together and screwed on the reel. Suddenly, cracks appeared in the clouds. Streaks of sunlight poured through, decorating the water like rhinestones on a shirt.

I hope the cracks in the clouds don't get bigger, let in more sun, and send the stripers deeper.

Wishing the answers to catching fish were as rigid as the state's vision requirements, I placed my bet on the sun coming out: I changed to a fast-sinking line and a white deceiver. I walked onto the lawn, pulled more than a hundred feet of line off the reel and stretched out the coils, about three feet at a time, out of my line.

I put on my stripping basket, retrieved the line, and walked to the end of the pier. The skyline of lower Manhattan came into view. Sunlight tinted some of the buildings. I thought of a Vermeer painting, of sunlight shining through a small window and falling on a woman's face. I wondered, though I knew it hadn't, if nature had learned from Vermeer.

From New Jersey the Manhattan skyline looked more awesome than I remembered. Though many of the buildings were of different eras, and though each building was of a different design, they all seemed to match, like mountains in a range. *Maybe the buildings, unlike nature's mountain ranges, match simply because of luck. How long does nature take to form a mountain range? Are ranges, like the Manhattan skyline, works in progress? Are ranges formed because nature, like humanity, spent thousands of years discovering, one by one, the techniques of engineering and construction? Maybe even nature, like me, is learning.*

In my mind I tried to fast forward a hundred years into the future and see how the skyline looked. I couldn't, even though I was wearing contact lenses.

I reached into my pocket, took out my long-distance fly-casting notes and visualized my casting techniques. Finally, I false cast, shooting more and more line and reminding myself to keep my elbow in. I hauled downward and then waited for a second. Keeping my shoulders still, I looked back. My loop was tight. I shot line and slowly drifted the rod lower, to about two o'clock. I hauled upward. When my line hand reached my rod hand, I cast forward, then hauled downward, shifting my weight all the way forward. Abruptly I stopped the rod. I let go of the line and, to reduce friction between the line and guides, raised the rod butt.

The front of my line formed a tight triangle, or wedge as fly casters called it. The wedge unrolled. My deceiver turned over perfectly and dived in the water. Proud, I looked for the 90-foot mark I had put on my line. The mark was just inside the rod tip. I had cast about 95 feet.

No, I wasn't cursed. *Maybe the murky, non-reflective water is just what it is, and not a symbol or metaphor of anything—and neither is my failing the eye exam.*

I retrieved as fast as I could and rewound my mind back to when I was forty-six and was sure I had landed a new job. But Fedex didn't call. Disappointed, wanting to erase another failure, I finished my third fishing article. A week later, an editor offered to publish it. Grateful, I told myself that, in spite of my failure to write the great American novel, I might as well try to write and sell fishing articles. Maybe then I wouldn't see myself as a failed writer.

But as I stood on the Hoboken Pier, my twenty or so published articles seemed way downstream of me. Upstream, I didn't see much of a future, and certainly not fatherhood, for me.

Again I cast about and then retrieved, remembering that I had never thought writing articles for local outdoor magazines would lead to writing memoirs and a fly fishing novel that reflected my emotional recovery. *Yes, the memoirs and book unfolded in my mind, little by little, by themselves, it seems. Could it be that Fedex didn't call for a reason? Did some unseen architect design the grand scheme of my life so I became a writer? But the idea is opposite of everything I believe: that the world is often random and violent, a tale, as Shakespeare says, told by an idiot.*

Again I false cast. Slowly, I began my forward presentation cast. I accelerated my fly rod, then abruptly stopped it and let go of the line. The fly rod seemed to come apart. *Did I lose the top half of my $600 rod? Another massive disappointment. The world always hits me when I'm down. Damn it!*

I looked up. The rod was there, all of it. I was grateful, until I saw that the small loop connecting the running line to the shooting head was broken. *Now I'll have to spend another thirty bucks for a new head.*

I put on my floating line, tied on a popper, and cast across stream, toward Manhattan. I retrieved, repeatedly jerking the rod tip up and down, pulling and banging my popper through the surface so that it splashed and sprayed water like a miniature speedboat. I reminded myself not to look at the popper, so if I got a strike I wouldn't pull the popper out of the striper's mouth.

Downriver, the Hudson flowed into the New York harbor. To me, it suddenly seemed amazing that a shallow, tree-lined stream in upstate New York could turn into a wide, deep, building-lined river. Was the Hudson, therefore, a reflection of the flow of humanity? After all, our knowledge supposedly deepened as generations flowed on. But the Hudson eventually flowed into the ocean and lost its shape and identity. *Perhaps if it knew where it was flowing to it would stop and wait, forever. But, like me, there are things a river can't cure, though in a few hours, when the tide changes, the river will turn around and go back, at least for a few hours. Is that a metaphor for the river flowing back into its character defects, the way I have? In many ways I'm like the river. I'm also flowing toward losing my identity, toward the final unknown. But before I reach it, will I somehow pull a Houdini and escape the dead-end in front of me? If only I could turn around and become a doctor,*

105

a lawyer, a forgiving son instead of an angry one. But like the banks of the Hudson, my past is shaped in stone.

Something, I saw, was wrapped around the bottom of the railing—my shooting head! A miracle, it seemed. Grateful, I unraveled the line and put it into my vest pocket. Thirty bucks—the cost of twenty knockoff cigars—saved.

Again I cast, this time about 100 feet! I retrieved.

A strike! I whipped my fly rod up and pulled down on the line. The striper pulled back hard. He was on. I let him run. He bolted upriver. I didn't try to slow or turn him. He circled, as if he didn't know where to go. Finally, he tired. Slowly, I reeled him close to the pier. I pointed the rod straight up, toward the sky, and grabbed the line. Hand over hand, I pulled the striper up. He was about thirty inches, a keeper, if I wanted to take his life. I took the hook out of the striper's mouth and dropped him back into the river.

I fished for about another hour, and though I didn't get another strike, I felt that, on this day in this small world of the Hoboken Pier, I had won, though I wasn't quite sure what.

I took apart my fly rod and screwed off the reel. *Breaking the line connector and having to change lines: could it have been meant to be? And what about my difficult childhood and my string of failures? Without them I wouldn't have later journeyed down the road of recovery. Perhaps, after this latest high tide of disappointment slackens, it will carry me to a new bend in the road of life. Yes, in a way the results of my physical were right: When it comes to seeing, at least into the future, my vision is blurred, for better or worse.*

I sat on a bench, lit a cigar, and watched the sun set. The smoke rose and blended into the marble-looking ceiling of gray clouds. The ceiling grew dark—it seemed eerie—but as the lights of New York grew brighter, as the city, like a night owl with a million eyes, came alive, it seemed to me as if it were sculpted from the same marble that covered the sky.

Wow! What a great day to be alive.

FLY CASTING WITH THE MAN OF LA MANCHA

The November sunlight shone through the blinds, telling me it was time to get out of bed. I tried but felt weighed down, as if I were a fallen knight, encased in heavy armor. Was I defeated?

I pulled the blanket over my head and hoped the approaching new year would bring sales of my book and money so I could finally travel to faraway fishing destinations. But the previous year had started with so much hope. What had it brought?

I thought of the vision test I failed, ending my hopes of becoming a court officer. I thought of all the mistakes in the first printing of my book—the proofreader had fallen down on the job—forcing me to have the book reprinted, at my expense: two major reversals and disappointments. Was I being punished, trampled on, like the knight Don Quixote, for dreaming of doing good deeds? If only the Man of La Mancha had succeeded in making the world a fairer place, then I'd be standing victorious. Wouldn't I?

I thought of the two magazines that had bought my articles but then folded, leaving my articles hanging out to dry, so to speak.

I thought of my disappointing new limo-driving job.

Three more reversals, five so far for the year, more than in most novels. And I still wasn't in the final crisis.

I thought of the GLX fly rod I had lost. I thought of the woman I drove from the army who reached out to me without telling me she had a boyfriend.

Seven disappointments in all, not quite as many as Don Quixote, but then the Don wasn't real. Maybe that's why he never had trouble getting out of, or even into, bed. But then again, Don rarely slept. Nevertheless, I wanted to be more like the Don, whether he was real or not. Besides, the day's weather was unusually mild, as if I were in southern Spain. A plus. An opportunity to fish and write myself a better plot-line.

I rolled out of bed, ready to battle with striped bass. Instead of armor, I took my fly-fishing equipment and headed out the door. Less than an hour later I walked to the north end of Roosevelt Island and into a scene as beautiful as any in La Mancha. I was in Lighthouse Park. The small park was named after a tall, narrow, stone lighthouse that I knew was not an evil giant.

I didn't attack.

Roosevelt Island is about two miles long, and two hundred yards wide. It split the East River, a major migratory route for stripers, in half. North of the island, the river again split, this time around Randall's Island. Half of the river turned eastward and flowed under the RFK Triboro Bridge—a bridge connecting three counties of New York City—and merged with Long Island Sound. The other half of the river hooked westward, and straightened and flowed out of my view and eventually, I knew, into the Hudson River.

I looked west, across the river, and saw about a half-mile of the Manhattan skyline. Most of the buildings had been built in the fifties and sixties, eras when New York architects were concerned with cost and function; so though few of the buildings were beautiful, they matched and, like bodies of water, merged to form a breathtaking skyline whose whole was infinitely greater than the sum of its parts. Another plus, in my book.

I turned, looked east, and saw a big, ugly Queens housing project. A minus. Unlike the different Manhattan buildings, all the project's dark brick buildings reminded me of identical, seven-story cardboard boxes. I wished I could be a real Don Quixote and obliterate them. But obliterating them wouldn't be easy, especially because they suddenly looked like giant soldiers—maybe from outer space—all wearing the same uniforms and standing in perfect formation.

Were they planning an attack, perhaps against the high-income buildings of the Manhattan skyline? Was I standing on another world's—perhaps a parallel universe's—battle line? Would the rules of the Geneva Convention apply?

They wouldn't have to. The housing project, I remembered, was home to many people. No matter how ugly it was, I didn't want to see it destroyed in battle. I wouldn't let it attack.

I set up my fly rod, tied on a white and green deceiver, and faced the housing project. The wind, not strong but steady, blew from Manhattan. To cut through it, I'd have to back cast parallel to the ground. Still, I was confident I'd cast close to 90 feet. I false cast, shooting more and more line. But my casts sagged, surprisingly. My loops opened wide. Had a new casting defect come out of the shadows to confront me like a villain? Or was I, like the pirated Don Quixote, trapped in a bad sequel? If so, I wanted out, or at least a fly casting coach, a Sancho Panza so to speak, to keep my casting on the straight and narrow.

I told myself I shouldn't have stopped practicing long-distance fly casting. After all, Don Quixote, up until his demise, didn't get burned out. Why not? Because he never let go of his impossible dream to save the planet, even before there was global warming. I, on the other hand, was tired of holding on to my dream of writing, of trying to change my sister and so many of the other people in my life.

I accelerated my cast, then abruptly stopped it and let go of the line. My deceiver landed only about 80feet away.

Disappointed, I quickly retrieved. Again I false cast. Again my casts sagged. I cursed. *After years of casting tribulations, after finally coming to believe I finally fixed all my casting defects, I just don't think I can deal with yet another reversal, another obstacle? But obstacles are meant to be overcome. Just ask Don Quixote.*

I thought back to the first chapter of my fly-casting adventures, to when I tried to understand fly-casting book after book, and then finally marched to a lawn and practiced casting, day after day.

I thought back to the second and third chapters, to when I tried to cast farther than 80 feet. But the fly often hit me or the tip of my fly rod. A reversal, unexpected. Why? I reread my fly-casting books and learned that I was lowering my rod hand at the end of the cast, and therefore pulling down the fly line. I returned to the lawn, and though I tried not to, I still lowered my rod hand. So four times a week, month after month, I experimented with every part of my cast—stance, trajectory, follow-through—but the fly still hit me. An obstacle I just couldn't seem to overcome. Downtrodden, feeling I was at a dead end, I trudged home, thinking that Don Quixote was foolish for trying to change the world, and that I was likewise foolish I was for trying to cast over 100 feet.

And so I wrote another failure into the story line of my life. A few weeks later, this new failure began to chomp away at my fragile self-worth. I somehow summoned the energy to get back on my fly-casting horse and resumed practicing. Then, by accident, I realized that when I cast with my elbow pointed almost all the way out from my body, my rod hand moved downward and pulled down the fly line.

Thrilled with my new discovery, I cast back and forth and watched my long loops tighten and streak like arrows.

During the next few months I overcame other fly-casting obstacles, and finally I cast 100 feet! I reached my impossible dream, for a while anyway, because as I fished on Roosevelt Island on the warm November day, I painfully accepted that some dreams, at least, are fleeting.

Seagulls dived in the East River. Bait fish were around. Maybe stripers were chasing them. I cast toward the birds. Again my line sagged. I couldn't reach my target. I cursed, then remembered I wasn't in a real-life tragedy, though like Don Quixote, I was a character in publications—my own, including my long-distance fly casting article. Maybe it held a forgotten solution to my casting defect. And if not, well, I still had faith the new obstacle was something I could eventually overcome. Instead of feeling defeated, I enjoyed fishing and feeling connected to the beauty all around me.

Four hours later, as soon as I got home, I started rereading my casting article. About a third of the way through, I read that if my back cast and forward cast formed an angle greater than 180 degrees, it meant I also stopped the rod too late, after it started unloading and losing power. If I executed my back cast parallel to the ground to cut through the wind, therefore, I had to execute my forward cast at the same angle, even though I was standing about five feet above the water.

I had rediscovered my solution! My story had a good ending.

Grateful, I closed my eyes and wondered why casting ten or twenty feet farther was so important to me. Were my casting experiments about more than distance?

Yes, they are also about my coming to believe in an ideal casting form, a form as absolute as a perfect literary form, like Shakespeare's sonnets, or as perfect as a law of physics, like Special Relativity. And why is that so, so important to me? Because, even though the world is riddled by random and often bloody turns of history, it is also unified by ideals that form a working order? If so, are ideals invisible and so hard to discover because what really gives them meaning is searching for them, and then using them to overcome defects and failures, and to connect to the good in the world?

Isn't that what spirituality is about? Perhaps an ideal, like a Manhattan building, is just a single part of a larger working order. And perhaps so am I, so when I tried, on my own, to impose my will, I almost always fell off my horse.

But that was then. Today, thanks to the ideals of recovery and fly casting—a Higher Power—I'm able to deal with disappointments, one by one, and to keep going, like Don Quixote.

Yes, I believe by the end of the book of my life, the good will outweigh the bad. That's not such an impossible dream.

BLOOD

I watched the Giants beat the 18-0 Patriots and win the Super Bowl. Thrilled, I thought of my father and wished he were still alive to share in their great victory.

I went to the bathroom. My urine was the color of red wine. Shocked, I remembered that my friend Howard had seen blood in his urine, and then learned he had bladder cancer.

I'm fifty-five. Aren't I too young to die? This can't be happening.

I told myself not to panic, to wait and see what happened in the morning. Besides, bladder cancer is usually treatable.

Somehow I slept through the night. In the morning I went to the bathroom, thinking everything would be all right.

It wasn't. I called my doctor. He told me to go to the emergency room. I listened to him, and then waited in a crowded room for about two hours. Finally, I was called.

A nurse sat at a desk and looked at the form I had filled out.

"Is your urine cranberry color?" she asked.

"No, darker."

"How dark?"

"The color of red wine."

"That dark?"

"Do you think I'd lie?"

"Is there clotting?"

"Yes. The clotting just started."

"Can you take this jar and give me a sample?"

I took the jar and went into the bathroom. I came out and said, "See, I told you: the color of red wine."

"I want you to take these forms to the admissions office."

"So I'm staying over?"

"We have to run some tests."

What if I have cancer and it has already spread the way my mother's did before it was discovered?

I walked into the admissions office. A heavyset woman greeted me. She asked for my insurance card, and then asked me to sign four or five forms. I did.

"I want you to walk past the nurse's station," she said, "turn left and walk down the corridor and into the emergency ward."

"Thanks."

The walls of the ward were green, the color of trees, bushes and grass, the color of the outdoors. The ceiling was white, the color of a cloud-filled sky. I didn't, however, see any connection between the ward and the beautiful outdoors; maybe because the ward didn't have windows and sunlight, unlike the bright hospital rooms my parents had passed away in.

A young nurse smiled at me. She said, "This is your bed. I need you to change into this gown." She had an Irish accent.

I said, "Did you ever do any salmon fishing in Ireland?"

"Do I look like an angler?"

"If you did it wouldn't be an insult."

"My brothers fished a lot, until they moved to America."

"That's sad."

"Yes, I suppose it is."

I changed into the gown, climbed into the bed, closed my eyes, and told myself to meditate. I thought of how fishing had helped me get through the deaths of my parents and through so many disappointments in my life. *Why aren't I scared? Am I in shock? Will fishing help me get through the final journey of my life? How I wish my parents were here. Who will worry about me now? Maybe I should call my sister. But she's been through so much. I shouldn't trouble her until I know more. Will I ever fish the Croton again? If I don't have cancer, how beautiful the Croton will look. How precious fishing will seem. Maybe the blood in my urine happened because I haven't enjoyed life as much as I should have, because I have often seen the bad instead of the good. If only it hadn't taken me so long to ask for help and to go into recovery. I've lost so much precious time.*

"Mr. Kadish." The nurse stood next to my bed. Alongside her was a short, young man.

"We're going to take you upstairs for a scan."

"What kind of scan?"

"A body scan."

"For tumors?"

"For precaution."

"Can I walk?"

"No, you'll have to stay in bed. Ernesto will take you up."

"In case I have to wait up there can I take my book?"

The nurse handed me my backpack, and I took out my copy of *In the Ring of the Rise*, a how-to book by Vincent C. Marino.

Ernesto wheeled me and my bed though the emergency room, and then down a long hallway. I asked, "Does this bed have GPS?"

"With all the hospital wings and hallways sometimes I think I need it." He spoke with a thick Spanish accent. I thought of the Spanish bait fishermen I had met on piers, and how some had ticked me off. Then I thought of how I had come to see the good in them.

I thought of how ironic it was that I, a chauffeur, was finally being driven by someone else, but in a hospital.

We stopped in front of an elevator.

I said, "You're a good driver."

"Thank you."

The elevator doors opened. A middle-aged man and woman—husband and wife, I guessed—were inside. They held hands, reminding me of the hand-holding couple I had seen when I fished from the old, 55th Street pier. The couple looked at me. Ashamed of lying in a hospital bed, I looked away from them. Ernesto pushed me into the elevator.

The elevator stopped at the next floor. Ernesto pushed me out.

I looked at the couple and said, "Take care."

"You too," the man replied.

Ernesto pushed me down another long hallway. *This hospital has more hallways than a big river has tributaries.* We reached a big alcove. The alcove reminded me of a wide pool. A woman wearing a white doctor's robe sat at a desk. A man wearing green scrubs sat next to her. He was about my age. He watched the TV that hung from the ceiling like a branch from a tree. On the TV was a boxing match, a replay of the Hopkins-Taylor fight.

I said, "I saw this fight,"

"Who do you think won?" the man asked.

"Taylor. But it was close."

"I guess you're here for the scan."

"I am."

"I'm Al."

"I'm Randy."

He looked at my book. "You're an angler."

"Yes. This book is a classic. I'm finally trying to become a real good trout angler, later than I should have."

"It's never too late."

"I wish it were so." For some reason, maybe because I wanted to be appreciated, maybe because I wanted an excuse for not being a very good trout angler, I told him that writing took up so much of my time that I didn't have much left over to devote to studying angling techniques.

"Wow, so you're a writer. What do you write about?"

"Fishing."

"I subscribe to *The Fisherman.*"

"You're also an angler?"

"Absolutely."

Is this a coincidence? Could there really be a loving force in the universe that connects anglers even in sickness and maybe in death?

I said, "I published my first article in *The Fisherman*. Funny, after twenty years of failing as a writer, I wrote a fishing article in three hours and sold it."

"Where do you fish?"

"All over, including the lakes of Central Park."

"Do you ever fish Little Neck Bay?"

"Actually, last year I fished it twice. I waded in."

"I fish there a lot. I have a boat."

"Do you fly fish?"

"No. I use spinning gear."

"Me too, sometimes. How do you like being a radiology technician?"

"I like it a lot.

I said, "If I were younger I'd consider becoming one too."

"But not everyone can become a published writer."

"More and more I wish I had listened to my mother and gone to law or medical school."

"A lot of people wish they were writers."

"Including one of my mother's doctors." Suddenly, I felt I was talking to a longtime friend. My loneliness vanished like a spooked trout. "How long will the scan take?

"About ten minutes."

Al wheeled me into a big room. In the middle was a strange-looking contraption. The contraption was a long table. Around the middle of the table was something that looked like a huge, white bagel.

"Don't worry," Al said. "It won't eat you."

"Thankfully I forgot to put on cream cheese."

Al laughed and then asked me to lie on the table and to listen for a voice that would tell me when to hold my breath and when to breathe.

"You mean this thing talks?"

"Not a lot."

"I wish I knew more anglers like that."

Al left the room. A few seconds later a synthesized robot-like female voice told me to hold my breath. The table moved forward, and I was rolled through the bagel. In my mind the bagel looked like an arched bridge. I pretended I was floating down a river. The table stopped, changed direction and rolled upstream. The machine told me to breathe, finally.

Three or four more times I was rolled upstream and down. Al walked into the room and told me the scan was finished.

I asked, "What happens next?

"The doctors will look over the scan, then fax the results down to the emergency-room doctor."

"How long will that take?"

"A few hours, maybe."

Al wheeled me back into the alcove. Ernesto waited for me.

"Wait a minute," Al said. He walked to the desk and wrote something on a Post-it. "Here's my e-mail address. Drop me a line in a few months and I'll take you fishing on my boat."

"Who knows if I'll be in any shape to go fishing?"

"Of course you will."

Easy for him to say.

A few minutes later I was back in the emergency ward. I looked at the clock. It was a little after eight. *Maybe I'll be home by eleven.*

I wasn't. It was midnight. I was hungry—no, starving. Again I asked the nurse for food. She told me for the third time she'd try to find something for me to eat, and then sat down at her computer.

I was angry. I was cold. I got out of bed and put on my long johns.

"Where you going?" the nurse asked.

"Nowhere. I'm just cold, as well as hungry. Is that all right?" *What's taking the doctors so long? Did they forget about me?*

"Be patient."

"I am patient—a hospital patient." I got back into bed and

pulled the sheets over my head. I couldn't sleep. I tried to imagine I was fishing a beautiful trout stream and listening to a gurgling river, and to singing birds and peaceful thoughts. Suddenly, I remembered that when I fished I listened, too often, to the resentments in my mind.

"Mr. Kadish," someone said.

I pulled the sheet away from my face.

The doctor stood next to my bed. "I got the preliminary test results back. I don't see anything significant. There is a small cyst on your kidney, but I don't think that caused the bleeding. Also there are some small lesions on your lung. They could be scarring from pneumonia or bronchitis. Did you ever have either?"

"Yes, I had bronchitis."

"The scans we did were without contrast. I think the next step is for you to get a scan with contrast, and definitely have your bladder looked into."

"You mean for cancer?"

"Many things can cause blood in the urine. Tomorrow I want you to make an appointment with my urologist, and I want Dr. Sherman to make an appointment for you to have a full scan with contrast."

Quickly, I dressed. Twenty minutes later I walked into my apartment. I looked at the clock. It was one-thirty in the morning.

I got into bed, my bed, and thought of a Grateful Dead song. *Yes, what a long strange day this has been.*

MY GREAT DEPRESSION

Two days after my "visit" to the emergency ward I met with a urologist who gave me a prescription for antibiotics and scheduled an appointment with me so he could look into my bladder—something I dreaded.

The next day I had a body scan with contrast. A few days later Dr. Sherman called and said, even though the results were encouraging, he wanted me to take a PET scan.

I asked, "If the results are so encouraging why should I take a PET scan?"

"Just so we're sure about the spots on your lung."

Dr. Sherman, it seemed, wasn't being honest with me. I understood he didn't want to scare me, but my having cancer was a real possibility. I didn't like the idea of doctors thinking they could fool me into believing I had nothing to worry about. Did they really think I hadn't heard of WebMD?

I hung up and thought of Robert and Thomas, and of the fear they must've lived with when they were diagnosed with cancer. Suddenly, I felt so sorry for them. Then I wondered if anyone would feel sorry for me. Again, I wished my parents, with all their shortcomings, were still alive.

That night I got a phone call from an old co-worker, Dan. Dan and I had never been close friends. I had trouble with his radical politics and with his bitterness. Dan was a failed artist, and I guess I was scared of becoming one too. Still, there was a bond between us: the Twelve Steps. Dan was a recovering alcoholic, though I suspected he occasionally fell off the wagon. (He often called in sick.)

121

"Randy, I ran into one of the guys you worked with. He told me you left Frank."

"Yeah, I had a run-in with his alcoholic son about a year ago. He wanted me to drive a car at night with one headlight out, up the Merritt Parkway to Fairfield, Connecticut. I told him no. That led to an argument. Then last week he told me his father was semi-retired, and that, since he was now in charge, it was my job to drive cars with one headlight out. I told him I couldn't do that, so he told me to leave. Dan, at this point in my life I just can't work for an active alcoholic. Sometimes I just hate them, though I know I shouldn't."

"I hear you."

"I have more news." I filled Dan in on my medical condition.

"I'm really sorry to hear that. It sounds like you're doing all the right things to take care of yourself. I hope everything turns out okay. I knew someone who was diagnosed with advanced bladder cancer fifteen years ago. They built him a new bladder. He's doing fine."

"That's the one thing I'm grateful for: Bladder cancer, as long as it hasn't spread, is treatable."

I remembered that, for an alcoholic, Dan was an exception: He listened.

"What are you going to do for work?"

"With my experience I'm not too worried. I've already applied to a few companies. Maybe things happen for a reason. After over twenty years of driving without a break, I think I need at least a short one, especially since Frank Sr. feels guilty about what happened and is paying for my health insurance, for now."

"I have medical news too," Dan said. "Ever since my hernia operation I've been having some trouble, so I have to go back and have a second procedure. It's nothing major. I won't even have to stay overnight in the hospital."

"When are you going in?"

"In a week."

Though I was concerned for Dan, I was envious. I wished I had his medical condition rather than mine.

We agreed to stay in touch. I hung up feeling glad that, in spite of our political differences, Dan and I had found a way to be friendly.

On the morning of my bladder exam I didn't feel very scared, probably because I was still in denial, the way I had been in denial about so many things: my fear, my vulnerability, and my lack of self-worth.

The bladder exam was negative. I didn't have bladder cancer. One more scan to go.

Also negative. I didn't have lung or any other type of cancer. Relieved, I was sure I'd feel great and finally leave my resentments and regrets behind.

I didn't, maybe because I again felt like a victim who, through no fault of my own, now had to start all over again at a new limo company.

Again the world seemed so unfair!

But I did start again and found myself surrounded with un-familiar faces. I felt lonely, like an outsider who didn't belong.

I made it through my first week at the new job when Bob, a guy I used to work with, called me. "I have bad news," he said. "Dan didn't make it."

"Didn't make it?"

"Yeah, he died of a heart attack on the table."

"What? He was only sixty-two."

"I know."

"How'd you find out?"

"Dan gave the hospital my name and number. I guess he had no one else."

To me it seemed so strange that just a week ago I possibly had cancer while Dan had a minor medical condition, and yet Dan had passed away, and I was fine.

I thanked Bob for calling. Yes, Dan had died a lonely, failed, bitter artist. I feared that so would I. More than anything I wished I could rewrite his story.

Within a few hours I sank into a quicksand of grief. Surprised at how deep and thick the quicksand was, I wondered if all my grief was over Dan.

Soon I realized how much I wanted to go back in time and make peace with my parents before they became ill. Again I wanted to deny my grief over losing them. I closed my eyes, and told myself that feeling grief was a sign of my now being strong enough to face and come to terms with it, and that soon my grief would run its course and retreat.

I opened my eyes and looked forward to my monthly therapy session.

It arrived, finally. I told Matt I'd gotten a clean bill of health.

"That's great news."

I told Matt about Dan, and then I spoke about my recent disappointments.

"And what does all that mean?" Matt asked.

"What do you mean?"

"Do you feel you caused all those disappointments?"

"No, that's what makes them even more painful."

"You do have good news: You're healthy. Why not focus on that?"

"My feelings are not a telescope. I just can't adjust them."

"Do you think it's in any way connected to your tendency to focus on the negative?"

Annoyed by the question, I answered, "I suppose so." I went on and told Matt how tired I was of being a chauffeur, of having to fight New York City traffic, of having to sit in a car by myself hour after hour, and especially of having to work for owners who never listened to me. "Chauffeuring was tolerable when I was pursuing a writing career, but that career has led me to a dead end walled with debt. I feel I've wasted the last twenty years of my life, and wish I had taken that job with FedEx all those years ago. Becoming a writer once seemed like a dream. Now it seems like a curse. I don't understand how, after my book got some great reviews, the reviews have just stopped. I'm so sick of writing and revising. Besides, I don't have anything new to say."

"Do you feel you have other career options?"

"Not unless I buy them in the stock market."

"You once talked about moving out West and driving a school bus."

"Do you think that's a real possibility?"

"You once thought it was."

"I feel like this conversation is going in circles." I looked at the small clock on the desk. The session was almost over. *I can't wait to get out of here.*

Matt ended the session by again reminding me that I had a tendency to focus on the negative rather than the positive.

Easy for him to say.

A half-hour later I walked into my apartment. Suddenly, my grief and disappointment spun like a black hole, and pulled me into a pitch-black depression. Nothing ever seemed to work out for me, I thought, and it seemed as if nothing ever would. I felt cursed and dreaded, as if it were the Black Plague, another ten years of driving a limousine. I was certain that, at fifty-five, I didn't have the possibility of finding a rewarding career. Wondering what the purpose of living was, I again read Hamlet's "To Be Or Not To Be" soliloquy. His words hit like George Foreman's punches. To me, living in misery seemed like a coward's way out. I didn't see how I'd be able to go to work the next day, or the next. My life suddenly seemed unmanageable. Grasping for something to keep me afloat, I finally reminded myself to stay in the day, but I couldn't, so I tried to stay in the hour. I couldn't. I tried to stay in the moment.

The moments moved like a river of molasses.

Somehow I made it through the next day of work, even though my black hole of pain spun faster and faster. My mind was bombarded with thoughts that I was trapped and all alone in the dead-end of my life.

Finally home, I thought, for the first time in my life, of the best way of ending it all. The thought of jumping off a building and mutilating my body didn't sit well with me, so I thought of taking an overdose of sleeping pills. But how could I get the pills? And how would I say goodbye? Easy: I'd write letters to my friends and to my sister, explaining why I had decided not to go on living. Yes, my decision would cause them, especially my sister, pain, but maybe, just maybe, they would find a way to understand.

How did Dan's death start a chain reaction of such dark feelings? How, with all my recovery, did I fall into my first severe depression? Was all my recovery, therefore, a waste of time? If only I could time-travel back, to before I was in recovery, then I could again repress and deny my pain.

But like a flowing river, I couldn't go back.

I thought of my sister, of how she had suffered from depression and had tried, several times, to commit suicide. I thought of how I never understood the pain she, and others, had lived with for year after year before modern-day antidepressants became readily available.

No wonder my sister, and Robert, and the bosses I've worked for became alcoholics and drug addicts. And what about all those people who don't have writing or dreams and have always had to work dead-end jobs to support families? How do they do it without being depressed? Yes, I've been blessed to have a dream, even though I haven't always been able to see it.

Finally, my work week ended. I spent my days off lying on my couch, watching movies and TV, and trying to numb my pain. I went to a Twelve Step meeting. Terribly ashamed of my great depression, I didn't talk about it.

Then I had to go back to work.

Like an angler wading upstream one step at a time against a strong current, I made it through, one moment at a time, another work week.

I stood on 57thStreet, waiting for a bus. I remembered how, whenever I shared my feelings with Matt, he always responded by asking me questions, and then telling me that all I had to do was change my thinking and I'd be all right. *Yes, thanks to him I always thought my feelings weren't valid and were therefore my fault.*

I got on the bus. The thought hit me: During all my years of therapy, Matt, no matter what I was going through, had never shown me the slightest bit of empathy.

A half hour later I walked into my apartment and meditated. *Yes, my depression, my thoughts of suicide, my lack of self-esteem, must be connected to my not receiving empathy. Yes, when I was a child and my mother raged and no one came to help me or my sister, we had no choice but to deny how much we wanted someone to tell us that her anger was not our fault, and to deny how much we wanted some empathy. And I've been in denial my whole life, but now, because of my recovery, I'm able, finally, to admit my craving. Has the final layer of my recovery been peeled? Am I now ready to have all my character defects lifted? If so, I should be grateful. In the past, when the other layers were peeled, I also felt pain. And my mother—yes, she too was in so much pain because her parents spent so much empathy on their dying son they didn't have any left for her. No wonder she raged. And my father: his parents were so self-involved they had little empathy for him. No wonder he denied his feelings. Yes, my cancer scare has changed me, though not in the way I expected. It has helped me admit that, by not understanding the pain of my sister and of others, I had caused them harm. Maybe the blood in my urine, like so many other seemingly bad things in my life, happened for a reason.*

And yet I still can't believe in a loving, active Higher Power. Is it because I'm afraid of being hurt again? Am I that vulnerable? No! I can choose to see myself as someone who's been through so much, and who has always gotten up, always kept using my pain to help me grow. Yes, my recovery, if I work it, will help me find a way.

I woke up the next morning and ate breakfast. My depression, it seemed, had lifted.

I went to a Twelve Step meeting and spoke about how my recent depression had changed me. After the meeting several people came up to me and told me how helpful my share was. Emphatically, they thanked me.

I thought, *Yes, perhaps I still have important writing to do, important amends to make. True, I don't see the solutions for my life right now, but in the past solutions have revealed themselves, not when I wanted them to, but later, unexpectedly, and always, I now see, for the better. And I see that my writings really are unified. Last fishing season I took so many notes for a new memoir. Finally, thankfully, I'm seeing how the memoir will end.*

SOLO ANGLER

At one time I saw myself as a solo angler, as someone who cherished fishing on my own schedule—starting and ending whenever I liked—without worrying about someone else's time card, so to speak.

And yet I also saw myself as a sociable angler, as someone who looks forward to meeting and talking to anglers, and then to moving on.

And I was a happy angler, until something changed, and I became bored with fishing. So I started taking stock of my life, and wondered if, because I was an outdoor writer, fishing had really been a way to an end: to writing and getting published. Could it be that maybe, just maybe, I was never really in love with fishing after all?

Again and again, as I still continued to fish, I asked myself this question, and then one evening I was returning from fishing the Croton River and got off the Metro-North train. A man about thirty years old asked where I fished. I told him.

"I've heard about the Croton. I've always wanted to fish it. How is it?"

"Not very long, but very beautiful."

"I'm Peter. This is my wife, Maria."

"I'm Randy. Nice to meet you."

We shook hands.

"I'd like to go up there with you sometime," Peter said. "I haven't fished since I moved to New York."

"It's better if we can go during the week when the Croton isn't so crowded."

"I can take a day off. I have a license and a DEP permit."

I gave him my card. "Send me an e-mail. I'm sure we can arrange something."

He stared at my card and smiled. "You're an outdoor writer."

"Yes."

"Impressive. I'll be in touch."

A few days later I received an e-mail from Peter. He mentioned he was an architect and could take off next Tuesday, before he started work on his next project. I suggested we meet in Grand Central Station and catch the 10:48 train. He agreed. Then I wondered, *Do I really want to spend so much time on a train with a stranger? Besides, maybe Peter is just using me as an unpaid guide. I shouldn't have let him rope me in.*

Monday night I didn't work late, luckily. The next day I met Peter in Grand Central Station. We bought tickets and boarded the train.

"I hope you don't mind," Peter said, "but I Googled you. I read 'City Angler' and 'Going Back Again.' Great stories. Your book sounds interesting."

"It's not selling well. The truth is if I had it to do over again I would have listened to my mother and gone to law school." Quickly, I decided I didn't know Peter well enough to tell him that lately I felt like a failure.

"I feel lucky to be an architect," Peter said, "but I'd feel even luckier if I didn't have to deal with office politics, and if I could fish during the week, like you."

I asked how Peter had become an angler. He told me his grandfather often took him fishing. "Fishing just stuck with me. When I was in college I used to work during summers as a guide for a lodge in Alaska."

"What was it like, being a guide?"

He filled me in on the good and the bad, and I wondered if I should one day become a guide. Soon the conversation drifted to the kind of architecture he designed and liked. He and I both liked pre- and turn-of-the 20thcentury architecture. Suddenly, it occurred to me our conversation was flowing like a meandering stream. Feeling as if I had known Peter for years, I was glad I had agreed to fish with him.

We were in Croton Falls before I knew it.

I said, "This is the whole town, all one-quarter of a block of it."

We walked through the parking lot and reached the foot-bridge. Below us was the East Branch of the Croton. I said, "The East Branch flows out of the top of a dam and is warmer than the West Branch, which holds mostly wild trout. Sadly, poachers are now taking a lot of fish. The West Branch is only about a mile long. It has three different sections"

We reached the big street intersection. I pointed left. "About a hundred yards down this road is the lower section. It's a long, slow-moving pool. I don't fish it much because both banks are lined with thick, thorny bushes that make it hard for an angler to get in and out of the stream."

We continued down Croton Falls Road. I told Peter that the middle and upper sections were lined with trees and a walking path. "The middle section is a string of riffles, runs and pools. The upper section is a long, not-too-fast run. Let's start upstream, near the dam."

"Okay."

We walked to Bridge Pool. I said, "Look down."

About twenty rainbows were scattered in the pool.

Peter looked upstream. "Wow, a little island. Beautiful."

"The riffles below the island are called Hal's Hole. He's a guy who used to fish this river almost every time I came up here. He's a great nymph angler. He's in my story 'City Angler.' I changed his name, though."

We climbed down to the river bank and followed the path up-stream. The sound of the crashing water coming out of the dam got louder and louder, and in my mind I heard the sound of an engine. About a minute later the dam and the white, crashing water came into view, and in my mind I saw a drift of snow.

I said, "This is as close to the dam as we're allowed to fish."

"This river is beautiful. An architect couldn't have designed it any better."

"Remember the bitter old man in 'City Angler?' That's the log he was sitting on. It's amazing the log is still here after all the floods and all the years. I wish I were as durable."

"What about the old man?"

"I never saw him again. I've often wondered why. I just hope he's still alive."

We put on our waders and set up our fly rods.

I said, "We should fish different flies. What are you going with?"

"What do you suggest?"

"A caddis emerger. I'll start with a streamer. Do you want to fish upstream of me or down?"

"I guess I'll start a little down."

We climbed down into the stream and started fishing about thirty feet from each other, within speaking range.

"I guess we'll have to do a lot of roll casting," Peter said. He roll cast three-quarters downstream, and then so did I.

Suddenly, like actors on cue, we stopped talking. I wondered if somewhere in the universe an angler's code said, "Anglers not talking when fishing is permitted."

No takes. Peter waded about ten feet downstream. So did I.

I said, "This is where the father taught the girl to fish in my story."

"You've given this place a lot of history."

"I just recorded it. Every time I fish this spot the thing I regret the most about the choices I made is not having kids."

"Maybe you will."

"Time has passed me by."

Peter smiled, stiffly, as if he didn't know what to say.

Another silence. We waded farther downstream.

We fished for about an hour. No takes. I said, "I hope you're not discouraged."

"Let's go after the trout in Bridge Pool."

We climbed up the bank, and followed the path downstream.

I said, "We'll have to fish the pool one at a time. You're my guest. You go first."

Peter waded into the pool. I sat on the bank.

The pool was almost twice as wide as the long run. Peter roll cast across the stream and let his emerger dead-drift downstream. On his third drift he hooked and landed a sixteen-inch rainbow.

Ten minutes later he landed another.

It was my turn. I tied on a caddis emerger. No takes. I asked, "What am I doing wrong?"

"Don't blame yourself. Keep at it and the takes will come."

Peter was right. A take, finally! I pointed the rod up and retrieved line. The rod pulsed once or twice, and then went dead. The rainbow was free.

I said, "I must've done something wrong that time."

"Downstream takes are hard, especially when we have slack in the line. What I like to do is try to delay a second, then sweep the rod to the side and pull in line."

"I'm going to try that."

A few minutes later, I got another take. I followed Peter's advice, and, after a short fight, I landed a beautiful rainbow. "Peter. I'm glad you're here."

It was Peter's turn again, and soon I lost track of time, but not of the number of fish we landed. Peter landed three more. I landed two.

I asked, "Do you want to fish the next section of the river?"

"Sure."

We walked downstream to the tail of Frustration Pool. I said, "The surface of the pool is always as smooth as glass. I like to start below the tail, so the trout don't see us, and make longer and longer casts, and then slowly wade upstream."

We waded into the tail, and, as if it were waiting for us, a caddis hatch exploded suddenly. We tied on matching caddis flies—size fourteens—and took turns casting upstream and twitching our flies to make it look as if they were trying to escape from the surface film. Our tactic, however, didn't work. The hatch ended as quickly as it had begun.

We headed to Garcia Pool. No hatches. We tied on searching nymphs, Hare's Ears.

I said, "Why don't you take the water just below the mouth. That's where I once landed a huge rainbow. We're lucky to have the whole stream to ourselves."

We fished for another two hours or so, slowly wading downstream. Peter landed another nice rainbow. I hooked a beast, but lost it just before I could grab it with my hand.

"That counts," Peter said. "If you had a net you would have landed it. Anyway, I got to start heading back."

I looked at my watch. An hour of daylight was left. Had I been by myself I certainly would have fished it, but surprisingly I didn't resent leaving the sunlight behind.

During the train ride back Peter told me his father was a psychiatrist who specialized in treating adolescents for depression, often with medication. I trusted Peter enough to admit I had been in therapy for many years but had never taken medication. "If I had, maybe I wouldn't have been so motivated to work out my defects, but then again maybe I would have enjoyed my life more. I know medication has saved my sister's life. Have you ever taken any?"

"Once, after I went through a breakup with an old girlfriend. Without it I don't think I would have graduated on time, and who knows, maybe it saved my life too."

Before I knew it the train pulled into Grand Central Station.

"Randy, thanks so, so much. You're a great, great guide. Let's stay in touch."

"Absolutely."

We got off the train, shook hands, and headed for different subways. I was sad that one of my greatest fishing days had come to an end. Then it hit me: The real reason I was tired of fishing was that I was tired of fishing alone. I wondered how I could make fishing friends and then I remembered there was a New York City fishing club. I Googled it, introduced myself on the bulletin board, and said I was interested in hooking up with other anglers.

A week later I made plans with two of the club's members to fish the lake in Prospect Park.

We met at the Parkside Avenue entrance to the park. John, who lived a few blocks from the park, was recently retired, I soon learned. He had been fishing the lake for over twenty years. Kyle was from out west. He had recently moved to New York because his wife was on a temporary assignment. He worked as a part-time consultant.

We set up our fly rods, and John took us for a long, three-mile tour around the lake, stopping at his favorite fishing spots so Kyle and I could make a few casts.

I said, "I had no idea this lake was so beautiful. I haven't been here since I was a kid."

"The nice thing about this lake," John said, "is that you never see the tops of buildings. You feel like you're really in the country."

We finished our tour of the lake at the long, white boathouse. I thought, *Another great fishing day, and I didn't even catch a fish.*

I said, "Maybe we can meet next week and concentrate on fishing the south bank."

"Fine by me," Kyle said.

"I'm game," John added.

I asked, "Are you guys interested in going up to the Croton?"

They both said they were.

I arrived home and e-mailed Peter, and told him about my experience fishing in Prospect Park. I asked if he wanted to meet me there one evening.

A few days later he still hadn't e-mailed me back. Surprised, I then remembered I once had trouble communicating. I wondered if I had said something wrong. In my mind I replayed our day-long conversation, but nothing I had said seemed wrong. My resentment toward Peter exploded like a caddis hatch. As the week passed, I tried to forget about Peter and to focus my thoughts on fishing with my new friends.

Again we fished the lake in Prospect Park. A week later we fished the Croton, and again I enjoyed acting like a guide. Next, we fished the Harlem Meer, then the Upper Twin Lakes on Long Island—but what had started out so promising, my fishing with friends, already soured.

Why?

John loved to disagree with almost everything I said. As for Kyle, he was a compulsive talker who hogged most of our conversations.

So, later in the fishing season, when Kyle told me he was moving back west, and John told me he was going back to school and would have less time for fishing, I wasn't disappointed. I looked forward, somewhat, to again becoming a solo angler.

Alone, I walked to Bridge Pool. I looked upstream, then down. No other anglers. The stream was all mine. Grateful, I put on my waders, set up my fly rod, and again tied on a caddis pupa. I waded into the pool, roll cast across and let my fly drift downstream, twitching my fly rod. Then, when the fly was directly downstream of me, I raised my fly rod and waited a few moments.

No take. I cast again. A take! I landed a rainbow.

Is this a sign of good things to come?

It was. I landed about ten more rainbows that day. Thrilled, wanting to share my success with someone, I called Robert as soon as I got home.

Robert, as I expected, third-degreed me about where and how

I had caught the fish. "When are you going again?" he asked.

"Next Wednesday."

"I'm going with you."

Wednesday morning, finally. As I got out of the shower my phone rang. The number on the screen was Robert's. I knew why he was calling.

"Randy, I'm really sorry—"

"You're not coming."

"Don't you want to know why?"

"I don't have time. I have to catch a train."

Again I was angry at Robert. On my way up to the Croton, I told myself I was a fool for hoping that he had morphed into a person who didn't break plans. I walked to Bridge Pool, imagining I was with a friend who didn't cancel plans or use me as an unpaid guide, but my imagination didn't whitewash my negative thoughts. I hoped that catching fish would. I decided, therefore, not to experiment with a new fishing technique. Again I tied on a caddis pupa. I waded into the pool and, as I had a week before, roll cast and let my fly drift downstream.

No take.

I cast again and again and again.

No takes.

How can this be!? Last week I caught so many fish using this same tactic. Why is the Croton betraying me and bringing me even more disappointment?

I changed to a streamer. No takes, still. My anger toward Robert and Peter boiled into a rage. I cursed them. I cursed the Croton. I closed my eyes. *Even though I have the whole river to myself, I'm hearing only the resentment in my mind. Why can't I hear and see beautiful sounds and images, and stay in the moment? My Higher Power, you are everything I learned in recovery. Help me, please. Grant me the serenity to accept the things I cannot change, and to find a way to forgive and to heal my hurt and stop my rushing anger.*

I climbed out of the river, sat down and leaned my head against a tree. I closed my eyes and asked myself if the Croton was capable of betrayal. After all, one of the fundamental truths of fishing was that a tactic that worked one day might not work the next. I asked myself if my feelings of betrayal were really about Matt. I had trusted him so much. *And long before Matt my parents hurt me deeply. Yes, they too betrayed me, and for so long I desperately wanted someone to tell me my parents' behavior was not my fault. But there was no one, and so to this day I've stuffed and denied my pain and my craving for empathy. No wonder after so much recovery, I still give other people power over my feelings.*

I opened my eyes and looked downstream. Some of the low, overhanging branches seemed to float on the water. Rays of sunlight bolted through an opening in the dense leaf roof, crashed on the water, and turned into bobbing flames. I remembered I had once described the sunlight as looking like sheets of hanging mist, and the sun-drenched leaves as stained glass in church windows. Telling myself I should try to come up with new images to describe the Croton, I reached for my pen and pad, but then I thought that maybe, on this day, I should let the beauty of the Croton speak for itself, without my interpretation of it.

But is that really possible? After all, ten minutes ago the Croton didn't seem so beautiful. Is the Croton therefore a combination of its own reality and of my perception? Yes, I think so. Then what changes my perception? My feelings, often negative ones I've learned I can change through prayer and meditation.

I stood up, waded back into the river, and cast. I retrieved line, varying my speed: sometimes fast, sometimes slow; and varying my pauses: sometimes long, sometimes short. Before long I lost myself and my resentments. *Are my retrieves a way to create my own time, my own reality, so that they will wash away, like a river flowing past me, the pain of my past, the hurt of my today and the fear of my future? After all, Einstein said time is relative. But relative to what? The speed of light, I know. But on earth the speed is abso-*

lute. *Are my retrieves really ways for me to stay in time, in neutral, unalterable moments that will never betray me because each moment is exactly like the ones before and after? Or maybe time is both relative and absolute. How? By connecting—in my mind, at least—the objective and subjective worlds?*

Again I cast. For some reason I thought of Kyle, of when he had invited me to his house for dinner. I thought of John, of when he took me on a long tour of Prospect Park. *Yes, maybe Kyle and John aren't perfect, but now I see the good in them. And I see the good in my parents and in my sister, and I feel empathy toward them. Isn't that the ultimate amends I can make?*

Two hours and no fish later I left the Croton, grateful for the lesson it had brought me. I looked forward to coming back, whether alone or with someone else.

Spring retreated into summer. The price of gas skyrocketed, and so the Croton beckoned more and more local anglers who didn't want to travel to the faraway Catskill rivers. In doing so, the Croton brought me more anglers to talk to, to help me feel as if I were part of a club; but when August advanced, the price of gas fell, and the fishing on the Croton slowed, so most anglers deserted it. Instead of looking forward to belonging, I again looked forward to having all the pools to myself, to experimenting with different fishing techniques. Yes, there were days I didn't catch a fish, but instead of frustration and disappointment, I felt connected to moments I didn't try to change; and in those moments I saw, all around me, the beauty of the Croton. I also saw and felt, inside me, the goal of becoming a better angler.

One day I fished the long run downstream of the dam. Again, I remembered that my disappointments in life had forced me to wade into the river of recovery and to learn how to communicate, how to forgive, and how to rise above my failures and character defects. And I remembered that a health scare had led me to understanding, finally, the deep pain my sister and others lived with.

I waded upstream toward the dam, the source of the Croton. I watched a rotating cylinder of silver water rush from the bottom of the dam, and turn into crashing, white foam, then into calm, clear water. The shape of water, like my feelings, was not absolute. Unlike time, it changed. I cast three-quarters downstream and watched my fly drift. When it stopped I waded a few steps upstream and again cast. Again and again I repeated the cycle: wading, casting. Soon I began to think of my wading as a symbol of my journeying upstream, into the future, and of my casting as a symbol for simultaneously staying in touch with my downstream, my past. Were my future and past therefore connected in each moment so I could never really lose all of myself? Or was it just a strained metaphor by a writer, me, who was reaching, straining for an answer that didn't exist, or was less than perfect, but still okay.

I looked to the bank, and in my mind I saw the old, bitter angler. I thought of how, because of his anger, he probably never saw the beauty I saw now. *So even if he were here with me, we'd be in different, perhaps parallel, universes.*

For some reason I thought of Sol, my mother's brother. In my mind I saw him sitting in his wheelchair. I wished he hadn't died—a death that changed the course of my life. But I couldn't change the past, I knew. I could only learn from it and see that his life, though broken off so soon after the start, still mattered.

Yes, I had to keep living, had to keep finding a way to enjoy a world that was less than perfect. Perhaps that was what the Croton was now telling me, giving me, the way it had given me other things I didn't know I needed: first, disappointment; second, a feeling of belonging; and finally, when I was at peace enough to enjoy them, pools all to myself.

Was the Croton in its way acting like a loving Higher Power, a Higher Power I couldn't always understand?

I looked at my watch. It was later than I thought. I had a train to catch. Slowly, I waded toward the bank, thinking that I couldn't wait for my next trip to the Croton, couldn't wait to see if a new fishing technique would help me land trout. Then I thought that it was the "if," the not knowing what would happen on the Croton, that was calling me back. Was it also calling me back to the joy of living? And was something else also calling me back? Yes, now it was clear: During my time on the Croton, nymphs had evolved into mayflies, and, without my knowing it, my feelings about writing and fly fishing had also evolved. I had fallen out of love with the work of writing and in love with the beauty of fishing, and though the beauty couldn't love me, it didn't matter because feeling love and empathy—something I could control—felt as good as getting them.

So I guess in a way I am no longer a solo angler. The way of spiritual recovery was always with me, and so was the way of the Croton and of all rivers.

I looked upstream, then down. I thanked the Croton for the lessons it had taught me.

EPILOGUE: AN ANGLER OF THE VAST WORLD

I live on Manhattan. That is not unusual. I fish on Manhattan. That is somewhat unusual. I also fish on Roosevelt Island. That is very unusual. Should it be? After all, the earliest New Yorkers—the Canarsie Indians, the Dutch and British settlers—all fished from the island; but then again, those people are of a world long gone in the river of time.

I am of today's world, and yet for most New Yorkers, even those who are dedicated fly anglers, Roosevelt Island, though just below the convergence of two great migratory routes for striped bass and blue fish—the Long Island Sound and the East River—hardly even exists. In fact, I've never seen another fly angler on the island.

Is it because the island is small, less than two miles long and two football fields wide? Possibly. Or is it because sophisticated Manhattan fly anglers have no interest in standing on concrete and casting with a railing in front of them? Probably, as I'm sure they prefer to stand in the historic rivers of the Catskills, the turquoise bonefish flats of the Caribbean, or the often-written-about rivers of Montana, Idaho and Alaska.

I can't say I blame them, especially because they have the bucks to fish exotic destinations. I do not. Like a tax cheat, I am paying a penalty, with interest, because I didn't listen to my mother and become a doctor or a lawyer. I chose a different course and listened to my dream—though elusive as a wild trout—and became a writer.

Where did the dream leave me? As someone who has never been paid more than $350 for an article, and who has recently been reduced to listing one of his e-books free of charge.

Yes, I have made some wrong choices in life. Am I bitter? I'd say disappointed; and so I often wonder what might have been. Often I accept that, in the scope of things and compared to those who have achieved success, I am, in the eyes of many, small, very small, just like Roosevelt Island.

What do I do about it? Make the best of a disappointing hand, even though I dealt it to myself. To do this, I manage to feel grateful to have Roosevelt Island as a subway-ride-away fishing destination, even though instead of hiring a well-paid guide, or fishing with well-educated fly anglers, I'm often fishing with bait fishermen, some of whom use broken fishing rods and barely speak English.

To help me get over my disappointment and feel more grateful, I decided to do some research and find out if Roosevelt Island had a history that would make the place seem—in my mind, at least—special, like the Beaverkill. Here's what I learned:

The Canarsie Indians, the earliest known owners of the island, called it Minnahanncock. The name means: "It's nice to be here." The Indians, using canoes, spears, and probably primitive fishing poles, fished year-round from the island. Craving its "crystal waters" and surrounding oyster beds, the Dutch bought the island in 1637. Because they raised hogs on it, they changed its name to Varcken Island (Hog Island).

From 1666 to 1674 the island passed back and forth between the warring Dutch and British. Finally, the British triumphed and awarded the island to Robert Blackwell, a prominent merchant and assemblyman.

After the Revolutionary War the Blackwell family tried to sell the now-named Blackwell's Island. Part of their real estate ad read: "It is remarkable for the number of fish and fowl that is caught there in different seasons."

They didn't get a buyer.

Finally, in 1828, New York City bought the island for $32,500, and soon started constructing what would become a world apart from the rest of the city. A lunatic asylum and prison were built. (Some prison inmates were Boss Tweed, Mae West, Billie Holiday and Dutch Schultz.) In 1856 the city opened a smallpox hospital on the island, and then a foundling hospital. In 1872 prison inmates built the island's most well-known structure: the lighthouse.

Eventually, the city decided to close the lunatic asylum and the prison, and to replace them with more hospitals. The island was renamed Welfare Island.

In 1955 a bridge connecting the island to Queens was built. Still, few New Yorkers visited or lived on the island. Wanting to change that, Mayor John Lindsay unveiled a plan to build several parks and many residential buildings on the island.

In 1973 the city decided, because of the island's limited vehicular traffic, to turn part of it into a haven where handicapped people could freely move about. To reflect this change, the city renamed the island after Franklin Delano Roosevelt.

Did learning this history help ease my disappointment? I think so, because now, whenever I walk the island's only street and pass its national landmarks, its hospitals, its new residential buildings and its new construction projects, I feel I'm in a place where time is different—slower perhaps—but also where the past, the present and the future converge like currents.

And so I often I think of the island's early anglers—the Canarsie Indians, the Dutch and English settlers—and feel I am following in their footsteps, even though I use high-tech graphite rods and advanced fishing techniques. Do I therefore catch more fish than the anglers I'm following? Probably not. They fished to eat. I fish for sport.

But to me anglers are anglers, connected by something that transcends time, equipment, technique, and even purpose, something I can't articulate but know is there and, like the migrating stripers and blues, something more constant than the changing anglers, inhabitants and names of the island.

And so I often stare at the East River, at its reflected sunlight that seems like a long diamond-paved path. I become so mesmerized I forget I have a name. But the path—because of drifting clouds blocking and unblocking the sun—comes and goes, like the anglers who fish from the island.

Soon, however, the sun, as it must, drifts lower in the sky, and the diamond path, as it must, seemingly sinks and then disappears. To me, the river with its newly layered ceiling of long pink and gray clouds is still beautiful; its new appearance is just a different take on the same world. Which world? New York? Roosevelt Island? Manhattan? But Manhattan and its skyscrapers and traffic-congested streets seem so far away.

And so I wonder: Where exactly am I? Yes, in a long timeline of anglers. How far ahead of me does that line begin? How far behind me will it end? Should I care?

Not sure, I looked up at the darkening sky. Several stars appeared, and I thought of how, when I'm on Manhattan, surrounded by all its bright, man-made lights, I rarely see stars and often forget that they are there, often forget that one day they will, like me, get old and then collapse and die.

But will they really? After all, a collapsed sky will form a time-stopping black hole that will explode and give birth to new planets. And perhaps one of those planets will give birth to life without wars and massive tragedies, and at least a small part of the universe will overcome its defects the way I, because of the black hole that exploded inside me, have strived to overcome mine.

Yes, there are eternal, predictable laws of the infinite universe and a renewing force that is so much greater than myself it will never betray me, and it will always dwarf all my resentments and disappointments. Because this force is so beautiful, is it possible that, as Newton said, only a God could have created it?

I know only that a vast world is beyond my vision and understanding, and yet in my mind I can visualize some of it and, in a sense, become a part of it.

I looked at my fly and retrieved it. Suddenly, I remembered part of a Second Step prayer, "I open myself to a power greater than myself."

And then I knew why, whenever I was on Roosevelt Island I felt so much bigger and so much more alive, as if I were of many times and of many worlds—me, an obscure, solitary angler.

No wonder I love to fish on this small, narrow island.

ABOUT THE AUTHOR

Randy is a native New Yorker. His writing has appeared in many publications, including *The Flyfisher, Flyfishing & Tying Journal,* and *Yale Anglers' Journal.* He is also the author of the historical novel, *The Fly Caster Who Tried to Make Peace with the World.* Much of Randy's writing is about the techniques of spin and fly casting, and about the spirituality of fly fishing. He often fishes the streams of Westchester, and the piers and lakes of New York City.

WITH THANKS

To Ernie Shulman and Sara Gallogly for reading my manuscript and helping me make my book better.

To all the people in "the rooms" for helping me come to terms and to feel as if I belonged.

To my parents and my sister for loving me and doing the best they could.

A NOTE ABOUT THE AUTOBIOGRAPHICAL STORIES

When does writing go from being a memoir to an autobiographical story? After spending much time thinking about this question, I'm still not sure. In several of the chapters in this collection, to tell a better story, I used composite characters, and I compressed or changed the order of events. Also, in *Where Rivers and People Converge* I changed Sol's toy from a clay soldier to a fishing lure. To me, these changes are, in the scope of my experiences, small and do not, therefore, take away from the so-called essence and truth of this book, which is about my spiritual journey of recovery.

www.ingramcontent.com/pod-product-compliance
Lightning Source LLC
Chambersburg PA
CBHW060930040426
42445CB00011B/868

* 9 7 8 0 6 1 5 7 0 6 7 9 5 *